Armageddon The Warning and the Promise

The Book of Revelation Made Plain and Easy to Understand

Larry Moench Davis

Copyright © 1999
Larry Moench Davis
5137 Joe Dean Circle
Ogden, Utah

ISBN 0-9670193-3-8
Library of Congress Catalog Card Number 99-67669

Table of Contents

Introduction

Introduction

It was never the author's intent to decipher "The Book of Revelation" word by word or line by line. It was written to give the reader a general understanding of each of the main topics that was shown to John by an angel of God. Once this general understanding is obtained, the reader can then peruse the actual scripture to search out additional nuggets of understanding. This book reproduces the entire text of the Book of Revelation as it was written using the King James Version of the Holy Bible. To facilitate ease of comprehension, a question and answer format was used with the corresponding scripture printed immediately following the topic.

1

The Vision Opens

As we enter the 21st century the world is asking the question, what will happen in the coming years? Of all the prophets God has placed on this earth, only one has been honored by God to see and report concerning what will happen between 2000 AD and the final coming of Jesus Christ. This prophet was called John. His report was written in a book titled, "The Revelation of St. John the Divine in the Holy Bible." This revelation has been given to help us know that, soon some great calamities will occur upon this earth. It provides a general outline concerning what will happen and is given as a warning to all those who will not follow God's commandments concerning the need to repent. This book was also given to help the righteous know of the great blessings that God has promised to all those who do His will.

Where did the information in the Book of Revelation come from?

It came from Jesus Christ and was given to John by an angel of the Lord who certified that the information was accurate.

> *1 The Revelation of Jesus Christ, which God gave unto him, to shew unto his servants things which must shortly come to pass; and he sent and signified it by his angel unto his servant John:*
> *2 Who bare record of the word of God, and of the testimony of Jesus Christ, and of all things that he saw.[1]*

Since this book was written approximately 2000 years ago, is the information in this book applicable to us?

Most of the prophecies outlined in this book will take place between 2000 AD and the final coming of Jesus Christ.

> *3 Blessed is he that readeth, and they that hear the words of this prophecy, and keep those things which are written therein: for the time is at hand.[2]*

Where was John told to send this information?

John originally addressed this information to the seven churches in Asia. However, it appears that the term seven churches, is used as a representative term to mean all churches

---

1. Rev. 1:1-2
2. Rev. 1:3

that belong to Jesus Christ. He tells the seven churches, in no uncertain terms, that this information comes direct from Jesus Christ, who died on the cross, was taken up into heaven, and will return again at some future time.

4 John to the seven churches which are in Asia: Grace be unto you, and peace, from him which is, and which was, and which is to come; and from the seven Spirits which are before his throne;

5 And from Jesus Christ, who is the faithful witness, and the first begotten of the dead, and the prince of the kings of the earth. Unto him that loved us, and washed us from our sins in his own blood,

6 And hath made us kings and priests unto God and his Father; to him be glory and dominion for ever and ever. Amen.

7 Behold, he cometh with clouds; and every eye shall see him, and they also which pierced him: and all kindreds of the earth shall wail because of him. Even so, Amen.

8 I am Alpha and Omega, the beginning and the ending, saith the Lord, which is, and which was, and which is to come, the Almighty.[3]

Where did John receive this revelation?

John was banished to the Isle of Patmos. It was there he received this information. He was told to write what he saw and send it to the seven churches in Asia.

9 I John, who also am your brother, and companion in tribulation, and in the kingdom and patience of Jesus Christ, was in the isle that is called Patmos, for the word

---

3. Rev. 1:4-8

of God, and for the testimony of Jesus Christ.
10 I was in the Spirit on the Lord's day, and heard behind
me a great voice, as of a trumpet,
11 Saying, I am Alpha and Omega, the first and the last:
and, What thou seest, write in a book, and send it unto
the seven churches which are in Asia; unto Ephesus, and
unto Smyrna, and unto Pergamos, and unto Thyatira, and
unto Sardis, and unto Philadelphia, and unto Laodicea.[4]

What did John see in the initial scene?

John witnessed a heavenly vision and the person he saw
was Jesus Christ in His glorified resurrected state.

12 And I turned to see the voice that spake with me. And
being turned, I saw seven golden candlesticks;
13 And in the midst of the seven candlesticks one like
unto the Son of man, clothed with a garment down to the
foot, and girt about the paps with a golden girdle.
14 His head and his hairs were white like wool, as white
as snow; and his eyes were as a flame of fire;
15 And his feet like unto fine brass, as if they burned in a
furnace; and his voice as the sound of many waters.
16 And he had in his right hand seven stars: and out of
his mouth went a sharp two edged sword: and his
countenance was as the sun shineth in his strength.
17 And when I saw him, I fell at his feet as dead. And he
laid his right hand upon me, saying unto me, Fear not; I
am the first and the last:
18 I am he that liveth, and was dead; and, behold, I am
alive for evermore, Amen; and have the keys of hell and
of death.[5]

---

4. Rev. 1:9-11
5. Rev. 1:12-18

What was John told to write?

He was told to write about the things he saw that pertained to his current day and also write of the things that will be shown to him concerning future events.

> *19 Write the things which thou hast seen, and the things which are, and the things which shall be hereafter;* [6]

What are the seven stars and the seven golden candlesticks that John saw?

The seven stars are leaders of the seven churches and the seven golden candlesticks represent the seven churches in Asia. Again, it appears that the seven leaders and the seven churches are used to represent all leaders and all churches that belong to Jesus Christ.

> *20 The mystery of the seven stars which thou sawest in my right hand, and the seven golden candlesticks. The seven stars are the angels of the seven churches: and the seven candlesticks which thou sawest are the seven churches.* [7]

---

6. Rev. 1:19
7. Rev. 1:20

2

Ephesus, Smyrna, Pergamos & Thyratira

Blessed is he that readeth and hear the words of this prophecy and keep those things which are written therein for the time is at hand. With these encouraging words John was ready to write a letter to each of the seven churches of Asia, but what should he say?

What information did Jesus Christ want John to impart to the church of Ephesus?

John was to inform the leader of the church of Ephesus that the information sent was from Jesus Christ. The Lord was aware of their good works, but that the Savior was concerned that they were losing their faith by not exercising the constant need to repent. He commended them for disapproving the actions of the Nicolatans. (This was a cult that believed that sexual immorality was not sinful because it only involves the physical body and not the soul. Their goal was to seduce the disciples of Christ into participating in pagan feasts and rituals involving sexual acts.) The Lord then gave hope by mentioning the blessings that awaited those who remained righteous to the end.

> *1 Unto the angel of the church of Ephesus write; These things saith he that holdeth the seven stars in his right hand, who walketh in the midst of the seven golden candlesticks;*
>
> *2 I know thy works, and thy labour, and thy patience, and how thou canst not bear them which are evil: and thou hast tried them which say they are apostles, and are not, and hast found them liars:*
>
> *3 And hast borne, and hast patience, and for my name's sake hast laboured, and hast not fainted.*
>
> *4 Nevertheless I have somewhat against thee, because thou hast left thy first love.*
>
> *5 Remember therefore from whence thou art fallen, and repent, and do the first works; or else I will come unto thee quickly, and will remove thy candlestick out of his place, except thou repent.*
>
> *6 But this thou hast, that thou hatest the deeds of the Nicolaitans, which I also hate.*
>
> *7 He that hath an ear, let him hear what the Spirit saith unto the churches; To him that overcometh will I give to eat of the tree of life, which is in the midst of the paradise of God.*[1]

---

1. Rev. 2:1-7

What information did Jesus Christ want John to give to the church of Smyrna?

John was to communicate to the leader of the church of Smyrna that Jesus Christ was the author behind the letter. The Lord was aware of their good works, and wanted them to know that; even though many were experiencing poverty, they were rich because they would become joint heirs with Jesus Christ if they remained faithful. The Lord acknowledged the existence of some Jews in the area who said they were Jews but followed after the works of Satan. He then gave hope by mentioning the blessings that awaited those who overcame even though it may require a martyr's death.

> *8 And unto the angel of the church in Smyrna write; These things saith the first and the last, which was dead, and is alive;*
> *9 I know thy works, and tribulation, and poverty, (but thou art rich) and I know the blasphemy of them which say they are Jews, and are not, but are the synagogue of Satan.*
> *10 Fear none of those things which thou shalt suffer: behold, the devil shall cast some of you into prison, that ye may be tried; and ye shall have tribulation ten days: be thou faithful unto death, and I will give thee a crown of life.*
> *11 He that hath an ear, let him hear what the Spirit saith unto the churches; He that overcometh shall not be hurt of the second death.[2]*

---

2. Rev. 2:8-11

What information did Jesus Christ want John to send to the church of Pergamos?

John was to write to the leader of the church of Pergamos and say that Jesus Christ was aware of their good works and was pleased that they had not denied the faith, even though it cost one disciple his life. However, the Lord was concerned because there were some in their congregation who followed the doctrine of Balaam, which promoted fornication and the eating of food that had been used in forbidden cult rituals. The Savior was also upset that some were participating in Nicolaitans rituals and warned of their need to repent or suffer the consequences. Hope was then given concerning the blessings that awaited the righteous who endured to the end.

12 And to the angel of the church in Pergamos write; These things saith he which hath the sharp sword with two edges;

13 I know thy works, and where thou dwellest, even where Satan's seat is: and thou holdest fast my name, and hast not denied my faith, even in those days wherein Antipas was my faithful martyr, who was slain among you, where Satan dwelleth.

14 But I have a few things against thee, because thou hast there them that hold the doctrine of Balaam, who taught Balac to cast a stumblingblock before the children of Israel, to eat things sacrificed unto idols, and to commit fornication.

15 So hast thou also them that hold the doctrine of the Nicolaitans, which thing I hate.

16 Repent; or else I will come unto thee quickly, and will fight against them with the sword of my mouth.

17 He that hath an ear, let him hear what the Spirit saith
unto the churches; To him that overcometh will I give to
eat of the hidden manna, and will give him a white stone,
and in the stone a new name written, which no man
knoweth saving he that receiveth it.[3]

What information did Jesus Christ want the church of Thyatira to know?

John was to explain to their leader that the information in
his letter came from Jesus Christ. The Lord knew their works
of charity and service. However, He was upset because there
was a woman (a self proclaimed prophetess) in their congregation who was seducing some members through fornication and
the eating of unclean food. The Lord wanted all the congregation to know that whoever committed fornication with her
would be under condemnation unless they repented. He commended those who were holding fast and confirmed the existence of more rewards to be given to the righteous, each according to his works.

18 And unto the angel of the church in Thyatira write;
These things saith the Son of God, who hath his eyes like
unto a flame of fire, and his feet are like fine brass;
19 I know thy works, and charity, and service, and faith,
and thy patience, and thy works; and the last to be more
than the first.
20 Notwithstanding I have a few things against thee,
because thou sufferest that woman Jezebel, which calleth
herself a prophetess, to teach and to seduce my servants
to commit fornication, and to eat things sacrificed unto
idols.

---

3. Rev. 2:12-17

21 And I gave her space to repent of her fornication; and she repented not.

22 Behold, I will cast her into a bed, and them that commit adultery with her into great tribulation, except they repent of their deeds.

23 And I will kill her children with death; and all the churches shall know that I am he which searcheth the reins and hearts: and I will give unto every one of you according to your works.

24 But unto you I say, and unto the rest in Thyatira, as many as have not this doctrine, and which have not known the depths of Satan, as they speak; I will put upon you none other burden.

25 But that which ye have already hold fast till I come.

26 And he that overcometh, and keepeth my works unto the end, to him will I give power over the nations:

27 And he shall rule them with a rod of iron; as the vessels of a potter shall they be broken to shivers: even as I received of my Father.

28 And I will give him the morning star.

29 He that hath an ear, let him hear what the Spirit saith unto the churches.[4]

---

4. Rev. 2:18-29

3

Sardis, Philadelphia & Laodiceans

J ohn, after being shown the information that the Lord wanted sent to the churches of Ephesus, Smyrna, Pergamos and Thyratira, was prepared to receive the information for the churches of Sardis, Philadelphia and the Laodiceans.

What information did Jesus Christ want the leader of the church of Sardis to know?

He wanted this leader to know that Jesus Christ was the

individual who caused this letter to be written. The Lord did know that some members were near death (with respect to activity in the gospel of Jesus Christ). Thus their works were not perfect in the eyes of God. Therefore, they needed to repent and renew their efforts and strengthen the testimonies of others who were near spiritual death. They were cautioned to be vigilant and hold fast so they would be ready when their time was finished. The Lord commended the few that were holding fast and then outlined more blessings to be received by those who attained the kingdom of God.

> *1 And unto the angel of the church in Sardis write; These things saith he that hath the seven Spirits of God, and the seven stars; I know thy works, that thou hast a name that thou livest, and art dead.*
>
> *2 Be watchful, and strengthen the things which remain, that are ready to die: for I have not found thy works perfect before God.*
>
> *3 Remember therefore how thou hast received and heard, and hold fast, and repent. If therefore thou shalt not watch, I will come on thee as a thief, and thou shalt not know what hour I will come upon thee.*
>
> *4 Thou hast a few names even in Sardis which have not defiled their garments; and they shall walk with me in white: for they are worthy.*
>
> *5 He that overcometh, the same shall be clothed in white raiment; and I will not blot out his name out of the book of life, but I will confess his name before my Father, and before his angels.*
>
> *6 He that hath an ear, let him hear what the Spirit saith unto the churches.*[1]

---

1. Rev. 3:1-6

What information did Jesus Christ want sent to the leader of the church of Philadelphia?

John was to affirm the information in the letter came from Jesus Christ. He knew their works and commended the members of the church for keeping His word and not denying His name. He again condemned those who say they are Jews but do not live by Jewish principles. Due to the good works of the general membership of the church, the Lord said He would protect them from the temptations of Satan. The Lord then told of several more rewards that would be given to those who overcome.

> *7 And to the angel of the church in Philadelphia write; These things saith he that is holy, he that is true, he that hath the key of David, he that openeth, and no man shutteth; and shutteth, and no man openeth;*
> *8 I know thy works: behold, I have set before thee an open door, and no man can shut it: for thou hast a little strength, and hast kept my word, and hast not denied my name.*
> *9 Behold, I will make them of the synagogue of Satan, which say they are Jews, and are not, but do lie; behold, I will make them to come and worship before thy feet, and to know that I have loved thee.*
> *10 Because thou hast kept the word of my patience, I also will keep thee from the hour of temptation, which shall come upon all the world, to try them that dwell upon the earth.*
> *11 Behold, I come quickly: hold that fast which thou hast, that no man take thy crown.*
> *12 Him that overcometh will I make a pillar in the temple of my God, and he shall go no more out: and I will write*

upon him the name of my God, and the name of the city of my God, which is new Jerusalem, which cometh down out of heaven from my God: and I will write upon him my new name.

13 He that hath an ear, let him hear what the Spirit saith unto the churches.[2]

What information did Jesus Christ want the leader of the church of the Laodiceans to receive?

John was to say that Jesus Christ told him to send the letter. The Savior was aware they were only lukewarm in following His commandments, because they were too rich and comfortable yet, in reality, they were miserable, poor and blind in things pertaining to the saving principles of the Gospel. They were to know that the Lord rebuked those He loved and if they would repent He would return to them. Again, more blessings were described for those who endured to the end.

14 And unto the angel of the church of the Laodiceans write; These things saith the Amen, the faithful and true witness, the beginning of the creation of God;

15 I know thy works, that thou art neither cold nor hot: I would thou wert cold or hot.

16 So then because thou art lukewarm, and neither cold nor hot, I will spue thee out of my mouth.

17 Because thou sayest, I am rich, and increased with goods, and have need of nothing; and knowest not that thou art wretched, and miserable, and poor, and blind, and naked:

18 I counsel thee to buy of me gold tried in the fire, that thou mayest be rich; and white raiment, that thou mayest be clothed, and that the shame of thy nakedness do not

2. Rev. 3:7-13

*appear; and anoint thine eyes with eyesalve, that thou
mayest see.*

*19 As many as I love, I rebuke and chasten: be zealous
therefore, and repent.*

*20 Behold, I stand at the door, and knock: if any man
hear my voice, and open the door, I will come in to him,
and will sup with him, and he with me.*

*21 To him that overcometh will I grant to sit with me in
my throne, even as I also overcame, and am set down
with my Father in his throne.*

*22 He that hath an ear, let him hear what the Spirit saith
unto the churches.* [3]

What is the most important information we need to glean from the writings of John to the seven churches of Asia?

Since these seven churches seem to represent all churches
of Jesus Christ, the problems experienced in each church represent the problems experienced in all His churches. Thus it is
important to review these concerns for our own sake. A summary of these offenses are listed below:

- Lack of faith and not being willing to repent.
- Willing to be led into fornication, adultery, and other im-
    moral conduct by seducing servants of Satan.
- Unwilling to strengthen our fellowmen who stray from
    the teachings of Jesus Christ.
- Unwilling to holdfast and endure to the end.
- Being lukewarm in obeying the commandments of Jesus
    Christ because we enjoy a comfortable lifestyle.

---

3. Rev. 3:14-22

• And, finally, being unwilling to accept rebuke and chas-
tening from the Lord.

Consequently, the Lord has stated that those who will not
keep His commandments and will not repent, will not be protected from the hour of temptation (tribulation) that will come
upon the whole world.[4]

---

4. Rev. 3:10

4

Vision of God, Elders & Beasts

J ohn, was shown the information that the Lord wanted
    sent to the churches of Sardis, Philadelphia and
    Laodiceans, He received the privilege of knowing that
God the Father was not a myth. That a supreme being really
does reign in heaven in all His glory. That heaven is filled with
His creations who worship and honor Him in response for all
God has done for them.

What happened after the angel gave John the information for the seven churches?

In a heavenly vision, John was allowed to see God the Eternal Father sitting on His throne in all His power and glory.

> *1 After this I looked, and, behold, a door was opened in heaven: and the first voice which I heard was as it were*

of a trumpet talking with me; which said, Come up hither,
and I will shew thee things which must be hereafter.
2 And immediately I was in the spirit: and, behold, a
throne was set in heaven, and one sat on the throne.
3 And he that sat was to look upon like a jasper and a
sardine stone: and there was a rainbow round about the
throne, in sight like unto an emerald.[1]

What did John see in front of the throne?

He saw twenty-four elders wearing gold crowns upon their heads, dressed in white clothing, seated before the throne of God. The twenty-four elders, from the seven churches, seem to represent all elders who have distinguished themselves by the manner in which they have carried out the work of the ministry. He also saw seven lamps of fire which represent the seven leaders of the seven churches.

4 And round about the throne were four and twenty seats:
and upon the seats I saw four and twenty elders sitting,
clothed in white raiment; and they had on their heads
crowns of gold.
5 And out of the throne proceeded lightnings and
thunderings and voices: and there were seven lamps of
fire burning before the throne, which are the seven Spirits
of God.[2]

What else did John see around the throne?

He saw four beasts near the throne of God worshipping their creator. These four living creatures, the lion, the calf, the man, and the eagle–though individual beasts–appear to symbolize

1. Rev. 4:1-3
2. Rev. 4:4-5

the different species that God created. They all worshiped God in response to the joy they received in being allowed to be part of the creation and developmental process.

> 6 And before the throne there was a sea of glass like unto crystal: and in the midst of the throne, and round about the throne, were four beasts full of eyes before and behind.
>
> 7 And the first beast was like a lion, and the second beast like a calf, and the third beast had a face as a man, and the fourth beast was like a flying eagle.
>
> 8 And the four beasts had each of them six wings about him; and they were full of eyes within: and they rest not day and night, saying, Holy, holy, holy, Lord God Almighty, which was, and is, and is to come.
>
> 9 And when those beasts give glory and honour and thanks to him that sat on the throne, who liveth for ever and ever,
>
> 10 The four and twenty elders fall down before him that sat on the throne, and worship him that liveth for ever and ever, and cast their crowns before the throne, saying,
>
> 11 Thou art worthy, O Lord, to receive glory and honour and power: for thou hast created all things, and for thy pleasure they are and were created.[3]

---

3. Rev. 4:6-11

5

Acceptance of Book by Jesus Christ

W hat a great honor it must have been for John to actually see God the Father in His heavenly realm. But John is about to see that those who are near the throne are very concerned about a book that God is holding in hand.

John saw that God the Father had a book in His right hand that was sealed with seven seals. An angel asked if there was anyone worthy to open the book. Just when it appeared that no one was qualified, Jesus Christ stepped forward and took the book from the hand of Heavenly Father. A great sense of joy permeated throughout the gathering that the Savior was quali-fied to open the book.

> *1 And I saw in the right hand of him that sat on the throne a book written within and on the backside, sealed with seven seals.*
> *2 And I saw a strong angel proclaiming with a loud voice,*

Who is worthy to open the book, and to loose the seals thereof?

3 And no man in heaven, nor in earth, neither under the earth, was able to open the book, neither to look thereon.

4 And I wept much, because no man was found worthy to open and to read the book, neither to look thereon.

5 And one of the elders saith unto me, Weep not: behold, the Lion of the tribe of Juda, the Root of David, hath prevailed to open the book, and to loose the seven seals thereof.

6 And I beheld, and, lo, in the midst of the throne and of the four beasts, and in the midst of the elders, stood a Lamb as it had been slain, having seven horns and seven eyes, which are the seven Spirits of God sent forth into all the earth.

7 And he came and took the book out of the right hand of him that sat upon the throne.

8 And when he had taken the book, the four beasts and four and twenty elders fell down before the Lamb, having every one of them harps, and golden vials full of odours, which are the prayers of saints.

9 And they sung a new song, saying, Thou art worthy to take the book, and to open the seals thereof: for thou wast slain, and hast redeemed us to God by thy blood out of every kindred, and tongue, and people, and nation;

10 And hast made us unto our God kings and priests: and we shall reign on the earth.

11 And I beheld, and I heard the voice of many angels round about the throne and the beasts and the elders: and the number of them was ten thousand times ten thousand, and thousands of thousands;

12 Saying with a loud voice, Worthy is the Lamb that was slain to receive power, and riches, and wisdom, and strength, and honour, and glory, and blessing.

13 And every creature which is in heaven, and on the

earth, and under the earth, and such as are in the sea, and all that are in them, heard I saying, Blessing, and honour, and glory, and power, be unto him that sitteth upon the throne, and unto the Lamb for ever and ever.

14 And the four beasts said, Amen. And the four and twenty elders fell down and worshipped him that liveth for ever and ever.[1]

---

1. Rev. 5:1-14

6

Opening First— Sixth Seals

S ince only the Savior was qualified to open this book John must have been very curious to know what was inside. Soon the angel showed him.

What was in the book that was sealed with the seven seals?

According to Archbishop Ussher's Chronology of the Bible, almost six thousand years had passed since Adam and Eve left the Garden of Eden (from approximately 4000 BC to 2000 AD). There is some evidence to suggest that the sealed book contained a description of a major happening during each one thousand year period since Adam and Eve. In other words, the first seal outlines a major event of the first thousand years, the second seal told of a major event of the second thousand years and so on until the seven thousand year point.

How do we know this interpretation is correct?

When the fifth seal was open, John saw great numbers of saints who were slain for the word of God. We know this occurred during the fifth thousand year period (1 AD to 1000 AD) because it was then that the Roman general Titus conquered Jerusalem and began a bloodbath that resulted in thousands of early saints being martyred over the next several centuries.

What event did John see when the first seal was opened?

John saw a person riding a white horse, with a crown on his head and armed with a bow going forth to conquer. This individual appeared to be a righteous leader fighting against the tyranny of evil, because white represents righteous and the crown represented a leader. This could be one of the righteous patriarchal leaders who lived during the first thousand year period (4000 BC to 3000 BC).

> *1 And I saw when the Lamb opened one of the seals, and I heard, as it were the noise of thunder, one of the four beasts saying, Come and see.*
> *2 And I saw, and behold a white horse: and he that sat on him had a bow; and a crown was given unto him: and he went forth conquering, and to conquer.* [1]

When the second seal was opened what did John witness?

---

1. Rev. 6:1-2

John saw a person upon a red horse. This person was given a great sword and had the power to take peace from the earth and men began to kill one another. The second thousand year period (3000 BC to 2000 BC) stands out as one of the most wicked times in the history of the world. It was so evil that God sent a worldwide flood to cleanse the earth so His future posterity could possibly be raised in a more healthy environment.

> 3 And when he had opened the second seal, I heard the second beast say, Come and see.
> 4 And there went out another horse that was red: and power was given to him that sat thereon to take peace from the earth, and that they should kill one another: and there was given unto him a great sword.[2]

What happened during the third seal?

John saw a rider on a black horse holding a pair of balances in his hand. Simultaneously he heard a voice speaking of wheat and barley. Blackness is symbolic of great suffering and the pair of balance and measure of wheat and barley indicate that this suffering is possibly caused from famine. Since the third seal dealt with the third thousand year period (2000 BC to 1000 BC) it is interesting to note that around 2000 BC Abraham's brother Haran died of starvation, causing Abraham to move to Canaan. It was also a famine that forced Jacob to move his family to Egypt where Joseph could feed them. This occurred about 1750 BC.

2. Rev. 6:3-4

> *5 And when he had opened the third seal, I heard the third beast say, Come and see. And I beheld, and lo a black horse; and he that sat on him had a pair of balances in his hand.*
> *6 And I heard a voice in the midst of the four beasts say, A measure of wheat for a penny, and three measures of barley for a penny; and see thou hurt not the oil and the wine.[3]*

What main event did John see during the fourth seal?

John beheld a person (representing death) riding upon a pale horse. This person was given power over a fourth part of the earth to kill with sword, hunger, death, and wild beasts. It was during the fourth thousand year period (1000 BC to 1 BC) that some of the greatest empires of the world such as, Babylonia, Persia, Meedes, and Alexander the Great of Grecia fought many wars resulting in much death and destruction.

> *7 And when he had opened the fourth seal, I heard the voice of the fourth beast say, Come and see.*
> *8 And I looked, and behold a pale horse: and his name that sat on him was Death, and Hell followed with him. And power was given unto them over the fourth part of the earth, to kill with sword, and with hunger, and with death, and with the beasts of the earth.[4]*

What happened when the fifth seal was broken?

What John saw occurring during the fifth seal or the fifth thousand year period (1 AD to 1000 AD) we have already dis-

---

3. Rev. 6:5-6
4. Rev. 6:7-8

cussed on page 29. Remember, when the fifth seal was opened John saw great numbers of saints slain for the word of God. Again, we know this occurred during the fifth thousand year period (1 AD to 1000 AD), because it was then that the Roman general Titus conquered Jerusalem and began a bloodbath that resulted in thousands of saints being martyred over the next several centuries.

> 9 And when he had opened the fifth seal, I saw under the altar the souls of them that were slain for the word of God, and for the testimony which they held:
> 10 And they cried with a loud voice, saying, How long, O Lord, holy and true, dost thou not judge and avenge our blood on them that dwell on the earth?
> 11 And white robes were given unto every one of them; and it was said unto them, that they should rest yet for a little season, until their fellow servants also and their brethren, that should be killed as they were, should be fulfilled.[5]

What will happen when the sixth seal is opened?

This is important, because the sixth thousand year period concerns us. This is the period we are currently living in (1000 AD to 2000 AD). As the sixth seal was opened John saw a great earthquake, the sun suddenly becoming black, the moon becoming as blood, the stars appearing to fall from the heavens and men scurrying about trying to find some protective shelter from the wrath of God. Later, in the Book of Revelation, the wrath of God is described as something that will happen at the time of the end. Apparently what John saw was the

---

5. Rev. 6:9-11

destruction that will occur to the wicked inhabitants on the earth just prior to the final coming of Jesus Christ.

> *12 And I beheld when he had opened the sixth seal, and, lo, there was a great earthquake; and the sun became black as sackcloth of hair, and the moon became as blood;*
>
> *13 And the stars of heaven fell unto the earth, even as a fig tree casteth her untimely figs, when she is shaken of a mighty wind.*
>
> *14 And the heaven departed as a scroll when it is rolled together; and every mountain and island were moved out of their places.*
>
> *15 And the kings of the earth, and the great men, and the rich men, and the chief captains, and the mighty men, and every bondman, and every free man, hid themselves in the dens and in the rocks of the mountains;*
>
> *16 And said to the mountains and rocks, Fall on us, and hide us from the face of him that sitteth on the throne, and from the wrath of the Lamb:*
>
> *17 For the great day of his wrath is come; and who shall be able to stand?*[6]

---

6. Rev. 6:12-17

7

Missionary Effort in Sixth Seal

I   f the initial scene depicted when the sixth seal is open is not the main event to occur during the period of 1000 AD to 2000 AD how do we know? And if it is not, then what is it John saw when the angel continued?

How do we know that the scene previously described is not the major event of 1000 AD to 2000 AD?

Because, as the vision continued, John saw an angel declaring to four other angels (who had the power to determine when this desolation would begin) that they were not to hurt the earth until an effort had been completed to locate and confirm all individuals who want to serve the Lord. Thus, it appears the main event that is to occur during the sixth seal, or the sixth thousand year period (1000 Ad to 2000 AD) is a global missionary effort to search out and seal the servants of Jesus Christ.

1 And after these things I saw four angels standing on the four corners of the earth, holding the four winds of the earth, that the wind should not blow on the earth, nor on the sea, nor on any tree.

2 And I saw another angel ascending from the east, having the seal of the living God: and he cried with a loud voice to the four angels, to whom it was given to hurt the earth and the sea,

3 Saying, Hurt not the earth, neither the sea, nor the trees, till we have sealed the servants of our God in their foreheads.[1]

Who will be involved in this missionary effort?

John saw that individuals from each of the twelve tribes of Israel will be ordained to carry out this effort. However, as the seven churches seem to represent all churches, it appears that these 144,000 could symbolically represent all the Lord's servants that are doing missionary work.

4 And I heard the number of them which were sealed: and there were sealed an hundred and forty and four thousand of all the tribes of the children of Israel.

5 Of the tribe of Juda were sealed twelve thousand. Of the tribe of Reuben were sealed twelve thousand. Of the tribe of Gad were sealed twelve thousand.

6 Of the tribe of Aser were sealed twelve thousand. Of the tribe of Nepthalim were sealed twelve thousand. Of the tribe of Manasses were sealed twelve thousand.

7 Of the tribe of Simeon were sealed twelve thousand. Of the tribe of Levi were sealed twelve thousand. Of the tribe of Issachar were sealed twelve thousand.

8 Of the tribe of Zabulon were sealed twelve thousand.

---

1. Rev. 7:1-3

Of the tribe of Joseph were sealed twelve thousand. Of
the tribe of Benjamin were sealed twelve thousand.[2]

How successful is this missionary effort?

John saw that this missionary effort would be so successful
that great multitudes of people from all nations would be gathered before the throne of God the Father and Jesus Christ to
receive white robes as a symbol of their faithfulness and to
enjoy the blessings available in the Kingdom of God. As a sign
of appreciation an outpouring of love was exhibited from this
great multitude.

> 9 *After this I beheld, and, lo, a great multitude, which no*
> *man could number, of all nations, and kindreds, and*
> *people, and tongues, stood before the throne, and before*
> *the Lamb, clothed with white robes, and palms in their*
> *hands;*
> *10 And cried with a loud voice, saying, Salvation to our*
> *God which sitteth upon the throne, and unto the Lamb.*
> *11 And all the angels stood round about the throne, and*
> *about the elders and the four beasts, and fell before the*
> *throne on their faces, and worshipped God,*
> *12 Saying, Amen: Blessing, and glory, and wisdom, and*
> *thanksgiving, and honour, and power, and might, be unto*
> *our God for ever and ever. Amen.[3]*

What is the significance of the white robes?

The white robes are a symbol of purity and righteousness.[4]
They are given to those faithful saints who have purified their

---

2. Rev. 7:4-8
3. Rev. 7:9-12
4. Rev. 19:8

lives, through the atonement of Jesus Christ, as determined by their willingness to obey His commandments. These are they who remain faithful even when they are subjected to great tribulation.

> *13 And one of the elders answered, saying unto me, What are these which are arrayed in white robes? and whence came they?*
>
> *14 And I said unto him, Sir, thou knowest. And he said to me, These are they which came out of great tribulation, and have washed their robes, and made them white in the blood of the Lamb.*
>
> *15 Therefore are they before the throne of God, and serve him day and night in his temple: and he that sitteth on the throne shall dwell among them.*
>
> *16 They shall hunger no more, neither thirst any more; neither shall the sun light on them, nor any heat.*
>
> *17 For the Lamb which is in the midst of the throne shall feed them, and shall lead them unto living fountains of waters: and God shall wipe away all tears from their eyes.*[5]

---

5. Rev. 7:13-17

8

Seventh Seal, First — Fourth Trumpets

It must have been very comforting for John to know that a worldwide missionary effort will take place and that, as a result, multitudes of people from all nations will be gathered unto God. But any joy he may have experienced was soon severely dampened by the news that he then received.

What happened when John opened the seventh seal?

John witnessed the main events that will happen during the seventh thousand year period (2000 AD until the final coming of Jesus Christ). As the seventh seal was opened John saw that there was silence in the heaven for about the space of half an hour. This could mean that the seven trumpets will not sound until after the half hour has elapsed.

What is the meaning of the term "about half an hour"? This is an important question because it tells us how much time will elapse following the year 2000 AD until the serious tribulations concerning the seven trumpets will begin to occur. Thus it could be one of several times.

First, it could be 30 minutes as we know it. Secondly, it could represent a half hour of the Lord's time, which would equate to about 21 years (the Bible says that 1000 years of our time is equal to 1 year of time where God resides.[1]) Lastly, it could be used as a symbol to represent a certain amount of time known only to the Lord. In any case, the Lord does not specifically tell John what time each event will occur. He does tell the sequence of events and this is very important because it can possibly give us some idea concerning how much time is left.

1 And when he had opened the seventh seal, there was silence in heaven about the space of half an hour.[2]

After the half hour period expires what did John see happen next?

John saw seven angels holding trumpets. These angels were in the process of preparing to sound their trumpets. How long is the time period concerning the seven trumpets? There is some evidence to support the belief that the seven trumpets may represent seven years.

In the book of Daniel, it suggests that in the last days the Lord will confirm the covenant with many for one week (biblical terminology for seven years). This possibly indicates that

1. 2 Pet. 3:8
2. Rev. 8:1

Israel will be given seven years to receive the covenant, repent of their sins and reconcile with God.[3]

> *2 And I saw the seven angels which stood before God; and to them were given seven trumpets.*
>
> *3 And another angel came and stood at the altar, having a golden censer; and there was given unto him much incense, that he should offer it with the prayers of all saints upon the golden altar which was before the throne.*
>
> *4 And the smoke of the incense, which came with the prayers of the saints, ascended up before God out of the angel's hand.*
>
> *5 And the angel took the censer, and filled it with fire of the altar, and cast it into the earth: and there were voices, and thunderings, and lightnings, and an earthquake.*
>
> *6 And the seven angels which had the seven trumpets prepared themselves to sound.*[4]

What happened when the first angel sounded?

John saw, as it were, hail fall from the sky followed by fire resulting in bloodshed. One third of the earth's trees were burned along with all the green grass. This first trumpet sound may very well announce the beginning of a nuclear war that could end up destroying the earth. What John may have witnessed were hails of nuclear bombs falling from the heavens resulting in pillars of fire mingling with blood. At first, it appeared this war would only involve one third of the earth.

> *7 The first angel sounded, and there followed hail and fire mingled with blood, and they were cast upon the earth:*

3. Dan. 9:24-27
4. Rev. 8:2-6

and the third part of trees was burnt up, and all green grass was burnt up.[5]

What did John see when the second angel blew his trumpet?

John saw a great burning mountain cast into the sea resulting in more bloodshed. He also saw the death of much sea life and the destruction of many ships.

As a nuclear bomb explodes over the ocean the resulting burning, billowing cloud appears to the untrained eye as a giant burning mountain. Radiation poisoning can easily account for the destruction of one third of sea life. And the ships destroyed could be nuclear submarines and surface ships carrying cruise missiles.

> 8 And the second angel sounded, and as it were a great mountain burning with fire was cast into the sea: and the third part of the sea became blood;
> 9 And the third part of the creatures which were in the sea, and had life, died; and the third part of the ships were destroyed.[6]

At the sound of the third trumpet what happened?

John observed a great star falling from heaven burning like a lamp. As it impacted the earth great damage was done to the earth's water resources. Multiple entry warheads, streaming down from an intercontinental ballistics missile, would appear just like a star falling from heaven. Any warhead exploding

---

5. Rev. 8:7
6. Rev. 8:8-9

near lakes, rivers, or water supplies would result in radiation poisoning. Some years ago a nuclear reactor in Russia malfunctioned. A large part of the underground water supply surrounding this area was poisoned. Interestingly, the name of this nuclear reactor was called Chernoble, which, in Russian, means Wormwood.

> *10 And the third angel sounded, and there fell a great star from heaven, burning as it were a lamp, and it fell upon the third part of the rivers, and upon the fountains of waters;*
> *11 And the name of the star is called Wormwood: and the third part of the waters became wormwood; and many men died of the waters, because they were made bitter.*[7]

What was depicted when the fourth angel sounded?

John recorded that the sun, moon, and stars were darkened throughout a third part of the earth. Again this is possibly symptomatic of nuclear warfare. As nuclear bombs explode over the earth, great pillars of fire, smoke and debris are blown into the sky. This can easily block out the sun, moon and stars from being visible over a third part of the earth.

> *12 And the fourth angel sounded, and the third part of the sun was smitten, and the third part of the moon, and the third part of the stars; so as the third part of them was darkened, and the day shone not for a third part of it, and the night likewise.*[8]

What does it mean when the angel said woe, woe,

---

7. Rev. 8:10-11
8. Rev. 8:12

woe to the inhabiters of the earth due to what will happen when the other three angels sound?

The word woe means intense suffering. Therefore, when the fifth angel sounds, this could signify that this warfare is about to expand, thus causing intense suffering, or great anguish to those involved.

> *13 And I beheld, and heard an angel flying through the midst of heaven, saying with a loud voice, Woe, woe, woe, to the inhabiters of the earth by reason of the other voices of the trumpet of the three angels, which are yet to sound![9]*

---

9. Rev. 8:13

9

Fifth & Sixth Trumpets

A t this point the war seems to be limited to an air borne conflict. It appears that John saw the war began to expand as ground forces started moving into place.

What event will occur at the sounding from the fifth angel?

John saw an angel come down from heaven. And with a key, given to him, opened the bottomless pit and appeared to unleash a dark Satanic military force upon all humanity.

> *1 And the fifth angel sounded, and I saw a star fall from heaven unto the earth: and to him was given the key of the bottomless pit.*
> *2 And he opened the bottomless pit; and there arose a*

*smoke out of the pit, as the smoke of a great furnace; and
the sun and the air were darkened by reason of the smoke
of the pit.[1]*

What type of warfare was John trying to describe?

In modern warfare, once the initial aerial attack is over, the various armies begin to move forward on the ground in mechanized armored vehicles. John was possibly trying to describe modern day armored warfare by using imagery from 1900 years ago. As the ground war begins it appears that the use of nonlethal chemical weapons could be the initial choice of torment. This type of chemical warfare is designed to immobilize its victims by causing vomiting, skin blistering, and nerve damage rather than a quick merciful death.

*3 And there came out of the smoke locusts upon the earth:
and unto them was given power, as the scorpions of the
earth have power.
4 And it was commanded them that they should not hurt
the grass of the earth, neither any green thing, neither
any tree; but only those men which have not the seal of
God in their foreheads.
5 And to them it was given that they should not kill them,
but that they should be tormented five months: and their
torment was as the torment of a scorpion, when he striketh
a man.
6 And in those days shall men seek death, and shall not
find it; and shall desire to die, and death shall flee from
them. [2]*

What specifically are these locusts, horses and

---

1. Rev. 9:1-2
2. Rev. 9:3-6

scorpions mentioned by John?

When describing the shapes of various mechanized vehicles, John could be comparing their images to that of horses, lions, and scorpions prepared for battle with breastplates of iron. What could look more like a lion that a tank painted to blend into a desert battlefield motif? What could more resemble a scorpion than a missile launcher with its missile angled skyward from the aft end of its launching platform? Is there a better way that John could describe armored helicopter gunships than by saying the sound of their wings was as the sound of chariots of many horses running to battle. And John even gives us the name of the behind the scenes commander as Abaddon, or the destroyer. Interestingly, one of the names Satan is known by is the destroyer.

> *7 And the shapes of the locusts were like unto horses prepared unto battle; and on their heads were as it were crowns like gold, and their faces were as the faces of men.*
>
> *8 And they had hair as the hair of women, and their teeth were as the teeth of lions.*
>
> *9 And they had breastplates, as it were breastplates of iron; and the sound of their wings was as the sound of chariots of many horses running to battle.*
>
> *10 And they had tails like unto scorpions, and there were stings in their tails: and their power was to hurt men five months.*
>
> *11 And they had a king over them, which is the angel of the bottomless pit, whose name in the Hebrew tongue is Abaddon, but in the Greek tongue hath his name Apollyon.[3]*

3. Rev. 9:7-11

What will happen when the sixth angel sounds?

John was informed the one woe is past, but two more were still to come. The first woe told of the suffering at the start of the conflict. The second woe, was a warning that even greater suffering will occur. John heard a voice commanding that the four angels which were prepared to slay a third part of men be released to carry out their assignment. With this statement, God seemed to be removing all barriers. Thus allowing the war to escalate to a point where a third part of men could be killed by fire, smoke and sulfur. Though the conflict starts out small, the way now seems to be open where many nations, through treaties and entangled alliances may be drawn into the war. Sadly, we are told that as devastating as this war is, men will still not repent.

> *12 One woe is past; and, behold, there come two woes more hereafter.*
> *13 And the sixth angel sounded, and I heard a voice from the four horns of the golden altar which is before God,*
> *14 Saying to the sixth angel which had the trumpet, Loose the four angels which are bound in the great river Euphrates.*
> *15 And the four angels were loosed, which were prepared for an hour, and a day, and a month, and a year, for to slay the third part of men.*
> *16 And the number of the army of the horsemen were two hundred thousand thousand: and I heard the number of them.*
> *17 And thus I saw the horses in the vision, and them that sat on them, having breastplates of fire, and of jacinth, and brimstone: and the heads of the horses were as the*

heads of lions; and out of their mouths issued fire and smoke and brimstone.

18 By these three was the third part of men killed, by the fire, and by the smoke, and by the brimstone, which issued out of their mouths.

19 For their power is in their mouth, and in their tails: for their tails were like unto serpents, and had heads, and with them they do hurt.

20 And the rest of the men which were not killed by these plagues yet repented not of the works of their hands, that they should not worship devils, and idols of gold, and silver, and brass, and stone, and of wood: which neither can see, nor hear, nor walk:

21 Neither repented they of their murders, nor of their sorceries, nor of their fornication, nor of their thefts.[4]

---

4. Rev. 9:12-21

10

Mission of John

As the war expands to include one third of the earth, John was suddenly shown a detailed picture of something else that was to happen between the sounding of the sixth and seventh trumpet.

What did John see concerning a book?

He saw a mighty angel descend from heaven, holding a little book in his hand. This angel declared that the time to repent and make things right with God was quickly coming to an end.

> *1 And I saw another mighty angel come down from heaven, clothed with a cloud: and a rainbow was upon his head, and his face was as it were the sun, and his feet as pillars of fire:*
> *2 And he had in his hand a little book open: and he set his right foot upon the sea, and his left foot on the earth,*
> *3 And cried with a loud voice, as when a lion roareth: and when he had cried, seven thunders uttered their*

voices.

*4 And when the seven thunders had uttered their voices,
I was about to write: and I heard a voice from heaven
saying unto me, Seal up those things which the seven
thunders uttered, and write them not.*

*5 And the angel which I saw stand upon the sea and
upon the earth lifted up his hand to heaven,*

*6 And sware by him that liveth for ever and ever, who
created heaven, and the things that therein are, and the
earth, and the things that therein are, and the sea, and
the things which are therein, that there should be time no
longer:[1]*

What did the angel tell John about the mystery of God?

John was told that when the seventh angel begins to sound
his horn an event will occur that previous prophets have curi-
ously referred to as simply a "mystery of God". More details
concerning this will be discussed in the next chapter.

*7 But in the days of the voice of the seventh angel, when
he shall begin to sound, the mystery of God should be
finished, as he hath declared to his servants the prophets.[2]*

When the angel gave John the little book what did he tell him to do?

After giving John the book, he told him to eat it, that in his
mouth it will be sweet as honey, yet in his stomach it will be
very bitter. Apparently, the book is sweet because it tells about

---

1. Rev. 10:1-6
2. Rev. 10:7

the blessings that God has in store for those that follow His
commandments to the end. And it is bitter because it describes
the terrible calamites that will happen to those who will not
repent and follow His teachings. John was then told that the
time would come when he would again prophesy before many
people.

> *8 And the voice which I heard from heaven spake unto
> me again, and said, Go and take the little book which is
> open in the hand of the angel which standeth upon the
> sea and upon the earth.*
>
> *9 And I went unto the angel, and said unto him, Give me
> the little book. And he said unto me, Take it, and eat it
> up; and it shall make thy belly bitter, but it shall be in thy
> mouth sweet as honey.*
>
> *10 And I took the little book out of the angel's hand, and
> ate it up; and it was in my mouth sweet as honey: and as
> soon as I had eaten it, my belly was bitter.*
>
> *11 And he said unto me, Thou must prophesy again before
> many peoples, and nations, and tongues, and kings.* [3]

---

3. Rev. 10:8-11

11

Seventh Trumpet

In addition to the mission that John will performed in prophesying before the world in the first days; it appeared that the angel showed him how some individuals will be protected when the need arises. And also, how the Gospel will be communicated to the Jewish people, living in Israel, before the seventh trumpet sounds.

What did John see concerning the temple and the people that worship therein?

He was told to measure the temple of God, the altar and they that worship therein. To measure, appears to mean, to keep from destruction. Thus the temple and the people that worship therein seem to be under God's protection. The outer court was given to the Gentiles, possibly meaning those who were left outside the temple are the non-faithful and thus subject to the appropriate judgments. Eventually, the righteous will need this protection because Jerusalem was expected to be treaded down for 42 months.

> *1 And there was given me a reed like unto a rod: and the angel stood, saying, Rise, and measure the temple of God, and the altar, and them that worship therein.*
> *2 But the court which is without the temple leave out, and measure it not; for it is given unto the Gentiles: and the holy city shall they tread under foot forty and two months.* [1]

What did John see concerning two witnesses?

This detailed view also occurs between the sixth and seventh trump. John was told of two witnesses who will prophesy, where Christ was crucified (Jerusalem)[2], for three and a half years (42 months) clothed in sackcloth and crying repentance unto the people. (It seems this may occur during the last half of the seven years allocated to Israel to reconcile to God.)[3] These two prophets will have power to smite the earth with various plagues until they have finished their testimony.

> *3 And I will give power unto my two witnesses, and they shall prophesy a thousand two hundred and threescore days, clothed in sackcloth.*
> *4 These are the two olive trees, and the two candlesticks standing before the God of the earth.*
> *5 And if any man will hurt them, fire proceedeth out of their mouth, and devoureth their enemies: and if any man will hurt them, he must in this manner be killed.*
> *6 These have power to shut heaven, that it rain not in the*

---

1. Rev. 11:1-2
2. Rev. 11:8
3. Dan. 9:24-27

days of their prophecy: and have power over waters to
turn them to blood, and to smite the earth with all plagues,
as often as they will. [4]

What will happen to these two witnesses?

John was told that the beast ascending out of the bottomless pit shall kill them. Their dead bodies will lie in the streets where Christ was crucified (Jerusalem) for three and a half days and then they will be resurrected (taken up into heaven). Their enemies will witness their resurrection and great fear will come upon them.

7 And when they shall have finished their testimony, the
beast that ascendeth out of the bottomless pit shall make
war against them, and shall overcome them, and kill them.
8 And their dead bodies shall lie in the street of the great
city, which spiritually is called Sodom and Egypt, where
also our Lord was crucified.
9 And they of the people and kindreds and tongues and
nations shall see their dead bodies three days and an
half, and shall not suffer their dead bodies to be put in
graves.
10 And they that dwell upon the earth shall rejoice over
them, and make merry, and shall send gifts one to another;
because these two prophets tormented them that dwelt
on the earth.
11 And after three days and an half the Spirit of life from
God entered into them, and they stood upon their feet;
and great fear fell upon them which saw them.
12 And they heard a great voice from heaven saying unto
them, Come up hither. And they ascended up to heaven in
a cloud; and their enemies beheld them. [5]

---

4. Rev. 11:3-6
5. Rev. 11:7-12

What will happen immediately following the resurrection of these two witnesses?

The angel showed John that the city will experience a great earthquake that will destroy one tenth of the city and slay many men. The remnant will fear God and give glory to Him. Thus the second woe is past and the third woe is coming very quickly, which entails even greater intense suffering.

> *13 And the same hour was there a great earthquake, and the tenth part of the city fell, and in the earthquake were slain of men seven thousand: and the remnant were affrighted, and gave glory to the God of heaven.*
> *14 The second woe is past; and, behold, the third woe cometh quickly.* [6]

What happens when the seventh angel sounds?

The seven year period, that appears to have been allocated to Israel, has now been completed. The two witnesses have been killed by someone the scriptures refer to as the beast. While these two witnesses were alive, they were given the power to hold the beast at bay. It was only when they finished their testimony that God allowed them to be put to death. It now appears the beast has triumphed, is now in complete control and will be allowed to trample the holy city for three and one half years.[7]

However, as the seventh angel sounds, John saw the twenty four elders conversing in heaven. They announced that with the sounding of the seventh trumpet the kingdoms of this world

6. Rev. 11:13-14
7. Rev. 11:2

would become the kingdoms of God the Father and His Son Jesus Christ. In other words, the time has arrived for Jesus Christ to reign.

> *15 And the seventh angel sounded; and there were great voices in heaven, saying, The kingdoms of this world are become the kingdoms of our Lord, and of his Christ; and he shall reign for ever and ever.*
> *16 And the four and twenty elders, which sat before God on their seats, fell upon their faces, and worshipped God,*
> *17 Saying, We give thee thanks, O Lord God Almighty, which art, and wast, and art to come; because thou hast taken to thee thy great power, and hast reigned.[8]*

What was John told would be one of the first things the Lord would do as He begins His reign?

John saw that the Lord's first order of business is to judge the dead and reward His servants, the prophets and the saints who fear God and serve Him. The second order of business will be to destroy those individuals who are destroying the earth.

> *18 And the nations were angry, and thy wrath is come, and the time of the dead, that they should be judged, and that thou shouldest give reward unto thy servants the prophets, and to the saints, and them that fear thy name, small and great; and shouldest destroy them which destroy the earth.[9]*

John now made another interesting observation. He saw that the temple of God was opened in heaven.

8. Rev. 11:15-17
9. Rev. 11:18

Why is this temple in heaven opened?

It appears to be opened to receive the resurrected saints who are judged, and found worthy to enter.

> *19 And the temple of God was opened in heaven, and there was seen in his temple the ark of his testament: and there were lightnings, and voices, and thunderings, and an earthquake, and great hail.[10]*

How do we know a resurrection will occur at this time?

Remember, John was told when the seventh trumpet sounds the mystery of God is finished.

> *7 But in the days of the voice of the seventh angel, when he shall begin to sound, the mystery of God should be finished, as he hath declared to his servants the prophets.[11]*

What do other prophets say concerning this mystery?

Paul taught that at the last trump the dead will be raised and we shall be changed. For this mortal must put on immortality.

> *51 Behold I shew you a mystery; We shall not all sleep, but we shall all be changed,*
> *52 In a moment, in the twinkling of an eye, at the last trump: for the trumpet shall sound, and the dead shall be raised incorruptible, and we shall be changed.*

---

10. Rev. 11:19
11. Rev. 10:7

53 For this corruptible must put on incorruption, and this mortal must put on immortality.

54 So when this corruptible shall have put on incorruption, and this mortal shall have put on immortality, then shall be brought to pass the saying that is written, Death is swallowed up in victory.[12]

What did Matthew teach about this mystery?

Matthew said that when the trumpet sounds, the angels will gather the elect from the four winds. That two people will be in a field and one will be taken and the other one left; that two will be grinding at the mill and one will be taken and the other one left.

31 And he shall send his angels with a great sound of a trumpet, and they shall gather together his elect from the four winds, from one end of heaven to the other.

40 Then shall two be in the field; the one shall be taken, and the other left.

41 Two women shall be grinding at the mill; the one shall be taken, and the other left.[13]

What did Paul say about this mystery?

Paul added that the Lord will descend from heaven, and the dead who served Christ shall rise first; then those who are alive shall be caught up to meet the Lord in the air.

16 For the Lord himself shall descend from heaven with a shout, with the voice of the archangel, and with the trump of God: and the dead in Christ shall rise first:

---

12. I Cor. 15:51-54
13. Matt. 24:31, 40-41

*17 Then we which are alive and remain shall be caught
up together with them in the clouds, to meet the Lord in
the air: and so shall we ever be with the Lord.*[14]

What did Jesus say about this mystery?

Jesus gave His disciples the parable of the ten virgins. This parable tells a story about a bridegroom who comes at midnight to reward His faithful virgins by gathering them unto Himself. All are believers in this lord, but five had been faithful in keeping oil in their lamps and the other five had not. When the lord came the five who were prepared were taken and the other five were left.

*1 Then shall the kingdom of heaven be likened unto the
ten virgins, which took their lamps, and went forth to
meet the bridegroom.*
2 And five of them were wise, and five were foolish.
*3 They that were foolish took their lamps, and took no
oil with them:*
4 But the wise took oil in their vessels with their lamps.
*5 While the bridegroom tarried, they all slumbered and
slept.*
*6 And at midnight there was a cry made, Behold, the
bridegroom cometh; go ye out to meet him.*
7 Then all those virgins arose, and trimmed their lamps.
*8 And the foolish said unto the wise, Give us of your oil;
for our lamps are gone out.*
*9 But the wise answered, saying, Not so; lest there be
not enough for us and you: but go ye rather to then that
sell, and buy for yourselves.*
10 And while they went to buy, the bridegroom came;

---

14. I Thes. 4:16-17

and they that were ready went in with him to the marriage:
and the door was shut.
  11 Afterward came also the other virgins, saying, Lord,
Lord, open to us.
  12 But he answered and said, Verily I say unto you, I
know you not.[15]

What do we really need to know concerning this event?

Apparently, this is the beginning of the harvest. The Hebrew harvest had three different stages. It began with the first fruits. The main harvest was next. Then the gleaning. This is where the poor were allowed to glean the corners of the fields. This resurrection of the elect is analogous to the harvesting of the first fruits.

It appears that in the last days there will be at least two major comings of Jesus Christ. When He comes to claim His elect He will come by himself in Glory and power. Possibly, only the elect will be able to see this awe inspiring event as it occurs, because only they will have the spiritual eyes necessary to discern their Lord and Savior, much like Stephen was the only one to see God as he was being stoned to death.

It is likely, the world will not witness the event, nor will the saints of Christ who were not faithful. Only their missing righteous friends and loved ones will provide any clue as to what has just occurred. Matthew helps us understand that this event will likely occur just prior to a major catastrophic event that is about to impact upon the saints.

---

15. Matt. 25:1-12

37 But as the days of Noe were, so shall also the coming of the Son of Man be.

38 For as in the days that were before the flood they were eating and drinking, marrying and giving in marriage, until the day that Noe entered into the ark,

39 And knew not until the flood came, and took them all away; so shall also the coming of the Son of Man be.[16]

---

16. Matt. 24:37-39

12

Role of Satan

The seventh angel has sounded, the beast may now believe he rules the world. However, John was shown that Jesus Christ will take control. The Lord's first action will be to resurrect the elect from the earth, probably to remove them from harms way. But this resurrection of the elect is only the first fruits. How will He bring about the main harvest? Instead of answering this question immediately the angel presented John with another historical thumbnail sketch showing the role Satan will play and how the main harvest will eventually happen.

Who was the woman John saw in heaven?

John now saw a woman in heaven and upon her head was a crown of twelve stars. As the following paragraphs are carefully analyzed it appears that the woman represented the Church of Jesus Christ.[1] This woman was pregnant with child and was ready to deliver. The child apparently represented Jesus Christ and the government by which He ruled.[2]

> *1 And there appeared a great wonder in heaven; a woman clothed with the sun, and the moon under her feet, and upon her head a crown of twelve stars:*
> *2 And she being with child cried, travailing in birth, and pained to be delivered.* [3]

Who was the red dragon?

In the heavenly vision, John saw a red dragon having seven heads and ten horns, and seven crowns upon his head. The red dragon is Satan.[4]

The seven heads are seven notorious world leaders (as indicated by the seven crowns), six are dead and the seventh is yet to come forth.[5] The ten horns are ten leaders of different nations who will come forth in the last days to help the seventh world leader reach his goal of world domination.[6]

> *3 And there appeared another wonder in heaven; and behold a great red dragon, having seven heads and ten horns, and seven crowns upon his heads.*[7]

Who are the stars of heaven?

John saw that the tail of the red dragon drew a third part of the stars of heaven, and did cast them to the earth. The stars are spirits that were cast out of heaven with Satan. Thus it appears

---

1. Rev. 19:7-8
2. Rev. 12:5
3. Rev. 12:1-2
4. Rev. 12:9

5. Rev. 17:10-11
6. Rev. 17:12-13
7. Rev. 12:3

that Satan has an army of spirits on earth to help him carry out his goals.[8]

In other words, in premortal life there was a conflict that caused Satan to be cast out of heaven onto the earth and he took one third of the spirit children of God with him.[9] The dragon (Satan) stood before the woman (Church) to devour her child (Jesus Christ and his government) as soon as it was born.

> *4 And his tail drew the third part of the stars of heaven, and did cast them to the earth: and the dragon stood before the woman which was ready to be delivered, for to devour her child as soon as it was born.*[10]

What happened to the man child?

John saw the woman (Church) brought forth a man child (Jesus Christ and His government), who was to rule all nations with the word of God: and her child was caught up unto God (possibly the result of the crucifixion of Jesus Christ).

> *5 And she brought forth a man child, who was to rule all nations with a rod of iron: and her child was caught up unto God, and to his throne.*[11]

Why did the woman flee into the wilderness?

The angel explained to John that the woman (Church) fled into the wilderness (place of protection) until the time was right when she could be restored to the world.

---

8. Rev. 12:9
9. Rev. 12:7-9
10. Rev. 12:4
11. Rev. 12:5

6 And the woman fled into the wilderness, where she hath a place prepared of God, that they should feed her there a thousand two hundred and threescore days.[12]

Why was Satan and his followers cast out of heaven?

According to Ezekiel, in premortal life, Satan tried to usurp the authority of God.[13] Because of this, there was a war in heaven. Michael and his angels fought against Satan and Satan fought against Michael's angels.

7 And there was war in heaven: Michael and his angels fought against the dragon; and the dragon fought and his angels,
8 And prevailed not; neither was their place found any more in heaven.
9 And the great dragon was cast out, that old serpent, called the Devil, and Satan, which deceiveth the whole world: he was cast out into the earth, and his angels were cast out with him.[14]

Why was Satan's communication with the Lord terminated?

Once the seventh trump has sounded, any communication that Satan may have had with God, for the purpose of accusing the saints, now appears to be terminated. For the accuser of our brethren is cast down, which accused them before our God day and night. Now this chilling final warning: Woe to the inhabiters of the earth for the devil is come down unto you, having great wrath, because he knows that he has but a short time.

---

12. Rev. 12:6
13. Ezek. 28:2, 13-15
14. Rev. 12:7-9

10 And I heard a loud voice saying in heaven, Now is come salvation, and strength, and the kingdom of our God, and the power of his Christ: for the accuser of our brethren is cast down, which accused them before our God day and night.

11 And they overcame him by the blood of the Lamb, and by the word of their testimony; and they loved not their lives unto the death.

12 Therefore rejoice, ye heavens, and ye that dwell in them. Woe to the inhabiters of the earth and of the sea! for the devil is come down unto you, having great wrath, because he knoweth that he hath but a short time.[15]

What will happen after the church is restored from the wilderness?

It was made known to John that after the Church is restored from the wilderness, Satan will again begin to persecute the saints. This is probably when the resurrection of the elect may occur. Satan may attempt to cast doubt and derision upon the veracity of resurrection and the Church, but will not succeed.

13 And when the dragon saw that he was cast unto the earth, he persecuted the woman which brought forth the man child.

14 And to the woman were given two wings of a great eagle, that she might fly into the wilderness, into her place, where she is nourished for a time, and times, and half a time, from the face of the serpent.

15 And the serpent cast out of his mouth water as a flood after the woman, that he might cause her to be carried away of the flood.

16 And the earth helped the woman, and the earth opened

---

15. Rev. 12:10-12

her mouth, and swallowed up the flood which the dragon
cast out of his mouth.[16]

What will Satan do to the saints who are left behind after the elect are resurrected?

John was informed that Satan is wroth with the Church and will make war with the remnant of her saints, which keep the commandments of God and have a testimony of Jesus Christ.

17 And the dragon was wroth with the woman, and went
to make war with the remnant of her seed, which keep
the commandments of God, and have the testimony of
Jesus Christ.[17]

---

16. Rev. 12:13-16
17. Rev. 12:17

13

Role of Beast & False Prophet

J ohn received more information concerning the role each of Satan's leaders will play during the period between the sounding of the seventh trumpet and the final coming of the Son of God.

What did John see concerning the beast, the seven heads, the ten horns, and the second beast?

He saw a beast rise up out of the sea having seven heads and ten horns. The sea represents peoples, multitudes, nations, and tongues.[1] Therefore, the beast itself is a nation consisting of many people.[2] The seven heads are seven great world leaders.[3] Six of these national leaders are now dead, the seventh is the world leader that will be in power during the last days.[4]

---

1. Rev. 17:15
2. Rev 13:1, 17:15
3. Rev. 17:10
4. Rev. 17:10,11

The head, is the leader of this nation.[5] Interestingly, one reference will speak of the nation as a beast.[6] Then another reference will speak of the leader as a beast.[7] Apparently, when the leader and the nation act as one, the leader carries the title of beast. As explained previously, the ten horns are ten leaders of various nations that will lend support to the beast in the last days.[8]

> *1 And I stood upon the sand of the sea, and saw a beast rise up out of the sea, having seven heads and ten horns, and upon his horns ten crowns, and upon his heads the name of blasphemy.[9]*

How is the beast like a leopard, bear, and lion?

As mentioned previously, the beast is a nation.[10] John was told that this nation has the capability to destroy like a leopard, tear apart as a bear, and like a lion chew to pieces any nation who dares hinder its progress.[11] This is important, because a single powerful nation is normally compared only to one type of wild animal.[12] This nation is compared to three. Thus this nation has the ability to destroy with great precision and awesome power. Where will it get this great power? We learn here that Satan will give this nation its power and authority.

> *2 And the beast which I saw was like unto a leopard, and his feet were as the feet of a bear, and his mouth as the mouth of a lion: and the dragon gave him his power, and his seat, and great authority.[13]*

---

5. Rev. 13:3   8. Rev. 17:12-13   11. Rev. 13:2
6. Rev. 13:1   9. Rev. 13:1   12. Dan. 7:5
7. Rev. 13:12   10. Rev. 13:1, 17:15   13. Rev. 13:2

John saw one of the heads of the beast as it was
wounded to death, and the deadly wound was healed.
What does this mean?

There are many explanations that could account for this.
One possible scenario is that the head of this beast is a world
leader who could come to power in the last days. He could rise
to power over that great nation that has the power to destroy
like a leopard, bear, and lion. During the course of his reign he
could receive a political wound that may appear to have killed
his political career. However, events may occur that will heal
this wound so that his political future may not be harmed.

If this scenario is correct, how would one account for the
fact that Revelation 13:14 mentions that this wound was caused
by a sword? Doesn't this indicate that the wound was inflicted
by a military weapon? Not necessarily, in Revelation 19:15,
Christ uses the terminology that His word is compared to a
sharp sword. So it is not unusual for the Lord to use the term
sword to mean word or written word.

In Revelation 17:8 this person is referred to as the beast that
was and is not and yet is. Revelation 17:10 provides more information by saying, there are seven kings: five are fallen, and
one is (in power during John's time) and the other is not yet
come; and when he cometh, he must continue a short space.
And the beast that was, and is not, even he is the eighth and is
of the seven.[14] How can this be? Here is one possible answer.

In the last days, an individual could be elected as the leader
of a great nation. He then becomes the seventh beast, after his

---

14. Rev. 17:10-11

term of office expires, he steps down for a while and then runs for this office and is reelected. Thus he could fulfill the prophesy by becoming the eighth world leader, but was still the seventh.

> 3 And I saw one of his heads as it were wounded to death; and his deadly wound was healed: and all the world wondered after the beast.[15]

Who will worship the dragon and the beast?

John saw that most of the world will unknowingly worship Satan because of the power he gives to this leader. Many will say no one is like this man, who can win against him.

> 4 And they worshipped the dragon which gave power unto the beast: and they worshipped the beast, saying, Who is like unto the beast? Who is able to make war with him?[16]

What do the words, "Speaking great things and blasphemies" mean?

John saw that this leader may be given the ability to make great speeches. Though he may appear to be religious, his actions will blaspheme the teachings of Jesus Christ. This world leader will continue his power for 42 months. Thus he could likely be in power before the angel sounds the seventh trumpet and may be given authority to remain in power for 42 months after the seventh angel sounds.

---

15. Rev. 13:3
16. Rev. 13:4

> 5 And there was given unto him a mouth speaking great
> things and blasphemies; and power was given unto him
> to continue forty and two months.[17]

What specifically will this beast do to blaspheme God?

John saw that this leader, though he will initially pretend to be religious, will eventually blaspheme the name of God, and all the saints that dwell in heaven by desecrating His sacred tabernacle.

> 6 And he opened his mouth in blasphemy against God,
> to blaspheme his name, and his tabernacle, and them that
> dwell in heaven.[18]

Why will the Lord allow this beast to make war with the saints?

The angel explained to John that since the Lord is now in power He may allow this evil person to carry out his will. Therefore the Lord appears to let the leader make war with the saints and to overcome them. There is a very good reason why God may allow this to happen. That reason will be discussed in the next chapter. Eventually the Lord will allow this leader to have power over all the people of every nation.

> 7 And it was given unto him to make war with the saints,
> and to overcome them: and power was given him over
> all kindreds, and tongues, and nations.[19]

---

17. Rev. 13:5
18. Rev. 13:6
19. Rev. 13:7

Who will worship this beast?

John was told that the people who live on the earth who will worship this leader are those whose names are not written in the book of life. If a person does not have his name written in the book of life, he will not be able to return to where God resides.[20]

> 8 And all that dwell upon the earth shall worship him, whose names are not written in the book of life of the Lamb slain from the foundation of the world.[21]

What is meant by the saying, "If any man have an ear, let him hear"?

It indicates that the discussion just presented is extremely important and has hidden meaning that needs to be searched out.

> 9 If any man have an ear, let him hear.[22]

What is the meaning: "He that leadeth into captivity shall go into captivity, and he that killeth with the sword must be killed with the sword?"

It means, he that captures may experience captivity and he that kills may be killed. In the last days, God is in charge. He will fight the battles of the saints. It appears that the saints are not to lift the sword against their enemies. It would be better

---

20. Dan. 12:1
21. Rev. 13:8
22. Rev. 13:9

for them to die as martyrs than fight and possibly lose a martyr's heavenly reward.

> *10 He that leadeth into captivity shall go into captivity:*
> *he that killeth with the sword must be killed with the sword.*
> *Here is the patience and the faith of the saints.*[23]

Why do we need to know about the beast?

We need to be able to recognize the beast when he steps on the world stage. These are some of the clues to his identity. This leader will be known for the following:
- rise to power in the last days[24]
- lead a great powerful nation[25]
- receive a deadly wound to the head which will heal[26]
- world will worship him[27]
- world will say no one is like him[28]
- world will say who can make war with him[29]
- is a great speaker[30]
- blasphemes God by pretending to be religious[31]
- blasphemes God by speaking in His name[32]
- blasphemes God by desecrating His tabernacle[33]
- blasphemes the saints in heaven by desecrating their beliefs[34]
- has power to successfully war against the saints[35]
- is given power over all nations[36]
- is the seventh in a succession of seven world leaders, of which six are already dead[37]

---

23. Rev. 13:10   27. Rev. 13:4   31. Rev. 13:5   35. Rev. 13:7
24. Rev. 17:10   28. Rev. 13:4   32. Rev. 13:6   36. Rev. 13:7
25. Rev. 13:2-4   29. Rev. 13:4   33. Rev. 13:6   37. Rev. 17:10
26. Rev. 13:3   30. Rev. 13:5   34. Rev. 13:6

- is the eighth in a succession of eight world leaders,
  but is still the seventh[38]

Who is the second beast?

John saw another beast come up out of the earth with two
horns like a lamb but speaks like a dragon. It appears that this
individual is a wolf in sheep's clothing. It is possible that this
person is a renown religious figure who secretly turns traitor
and leads much of humanity to destruction as they unwittingly
support the first beast (world leader).

There is the possibility that this second beast is a woman.
The Bible tells us that long ago King David committed adultery with Bathsheba and she became pregnant. To keep the
world from discovering what really happened, David had
Bathsheba's husband Uriah killed in battle.

Later, the prophet Nathan chastised David and compared
him to a thief who stole another person's lamb. Thus, Nathan
compared the woman, Bathsheba to a lamb.[39]

Another clue that may indicate that this person could be a
woman is this: Whereas the first beast comes up out of the sea,
this second beast comes up out of the earth. The earth has the
ability to grow seed and produce life. A woman has the same
capability. Concerning the two horns, in Biblical terminology
a horn means a source of power.[40] The two horns could indicate two sources of power. One source might be the world leader
and the second source may be from a political movement that
she supports.

But why would John use the term "he" when referring to

---

38. Rev. 17:11
39. 2 Sam. 12:1-10
40. Dan. 8:7

this second beast? It may be that John only saw a beast and that the Lord did not want John to know the gender of the beast. The term, speaks as a dragon may indicate that while she portrays herself as a woman, her speech is closer to the type of vocabulary that Satan would use. This beast is also referred to as a false prophet.[41] This would indicate a propensity to commune with the spirit world in order to receive guidance and direction.

> 11 And I beheld another beast coming up out of the earth; and he had two horns like a lamb, and he spake as a dragon.[42]

How could this false prophet exercise all the power of the first beast?

It is possible that the false prophet is very close to the first beast, thus there could be a bond of mutual support and willingness to share knowledge and power. This would account for how the false prophet could exercise all the power of the first beast. It would also explain why the false prophet would make the effort to cause all mankind to worship the first beast.

> 12 And he exerciseth all the power of the first beast before him, and causeth the earth and them which dwell therein to worship the first beast, whose deadly wound was healed.[43]

---

41. Rev. 16:13
42. Rev. 13:11
43. Rev. 13:12

How does the false prophet make fire come down from heaven?

The first beast, as the leader of the nation's armed forces, has the power to call down firepower from aircraft, missiles, and heavy guns against any perceived enemy. Thus it is possible for the false prophet to do the same, because we know the false prophet can exercise all the power of the first beast.

> *13 And he doeth great wonders, so that he maketh fire come down from heaven on the earth in the sight of men,*[44]

How does the false prophet deceive people by these miracles and why would this person want the people of the earth to make an image to the first beast?

They could be deceived because they are not aware of the false prophet's ability to exercise the power of the first beast in making fire come down from heaven. Also, the false prophet may view the position of the first beast as a shared honor. Therefore, the more the first beast is worshipped, the more the false prophet could be revered and honored.

> *14 And deceiveth them that dwell on the earth by the means of those miracles which he had power to do in the sight of the beast; saying to them that dwell on the earth, that they should make an image to the beast, which had the wound by a sword, and did live.*[45]

---

44. Rev. 13:13
45. Rev. 13:14

How does the false prophet have power to give life to the image of the beast?

The first beast could make many televised appearances, in fact, most people may never see the beast in person, they might only see his image on the television screen. It appears that the false prophet may have the power to influence when the beast appears on TV, and what he may say. The false prophet could also orchestrate a movement to have all who will not worship the image of the beast put to death.

> *15 And he had power to give life unto the image of the beast, that the image of the beast should both speak, and cause that as many as would not worship the image of the beast should be killed.*[46]

Why would the false prophet want to cause all mankind to receive a mark so no one could buy or sell anything unless they had that mark?

This could be a way of staying in power. By determining who supports the first beast and who does not, one can eliminate the competition and then encourage the fence sitters to give their support to the first beast. This mark could be similar to a national fingerprint identification card or a national picture identification card.

> *16 And he causeth all, both small and great, rich and poor, free and bond, to receive a mark in their right hand,*

---

46. Rev. 13:15

or in their foreheads:
17 And that no man might buy or sell, save he that had
the mark, or the name of the beast, or the number of his
name.[47]

What is the meaning of the number six hundred threescore and six?

Scholars have been trying to figure this out for hundreds of years. The answer to this question will probably not be known until the beast himself declares the answer.

18 Here is wisdom. Let him that hath understanding count
the number of the beast: for it is the number of a man;
and his number is Six hundred threescore and six.[48]

What do we need to know about the false prophet?

We need to be able to identify this person so we will know when the false prophet arrives. Luke says that we can tell whether a person is good or evil by the fruit they bring forth.[49] This false prophet will be known for the following:
- have the outward appearance like a lamb[50]
- come up out of the earth[51]
- have two horns[52]
- speak as a dragon[53]
- exercise all the power of the first beast[54]
- cause all to worship the first beast[55]
- make fire come down from heaven[56]

---

47. Rev. 13:16-17   50. Rev. 13:11   53. Rev. 13:11
48. Rev. 13:18   51. Rev. 13:11   54. Rev. 13:12
49. Luke 6:43-44   52. Rev. 13:11   55. Rev. 13:12

- deceive all by means of miracles[57]
- have all make an image to the beast [58]
- give life to the image of the beast[59]
- cause the image of the beast to speak[60]
- cause all who do not worship the image to be put to death[61]
- cause all to receive a mark that no man may buy or sell unless he has this mark[62]
- propensity to commune with the spirit world in order to receive guidance and direction[63]

56. Rev. 13:13   59. Rev. 13:15   62. Rev. 13:16
57. Rev. 13:14   60. Rev. 13:15   63. Rev. 16:13
58. Rev. 13:14   61. Rev. 13:15

14

The Harvest Begins

T he following occurs after the elect saints are resurrected and before the final coming of Jesus. John
was shown a scene that takes place in heaven.

Who did John see standing on Mount Sion?

John saw Jesus Christ and with Him are the 144 thousand
righteous missionaries who appear to have come forth during
the resurrection of the elect.

> *1 And I looked, and, lo, a Lamb stood on the mount Sion,
> and with him an hundred forty and four thousand, having
> his Father's name written in their foreheads.[1]*

Why will there be joy in heaven?

When the first fruits of the resurrection arrive they worship

---

1. Rev. 14:1

Jesus Christ by singing a special song that only these elect of the saints have earned the right to sing.

> *2 And I heard a voice from heaven, as the voice of many waters, and as the voice of a great thunder: and I heard the voice of harpers harping with their harps:*
> *3 And they sung as it were a new song before the throne, and before the four beasts, and the elders: and no man could learn that song but the hundred and forty and four thousand, which were redeemed from the earth.[2]*

What is the meaning of the term "not being defiled with women"?

It possibly means that these individuals were faithful to Jesus Christ by being obedient to His commandments. They are virgins because they probably did not whore after the temptations of Satan. Thus it appears they earned the right to be the first fruits of the resurrection.

> *4 These are they which were not defiled with women; for they are virgins. These are they which follow the Lamb whithersoever he goeth. These were redeemed from among men, being the firstfruits unto God and to the Lamb.*
> *5 And in their mouth was found no guile: for they are without fault before the throne of God.[3]*

Will a final missionary effort be launched after the elect are resurrected, but before the final coming of Jesus Christ?

---

2. Rev. 14:2-3
3. Rev. 14:4-5

After the seventh angel has sounded (for the hour of his judgment has come) and the elect are resurrected, this may likely cause a renewed interest for those who hope to follow their friends and loved ones. Also, those who are really curious will probably want to find out what happened by learning more about the gospel of Jesus Christ. Thus a last ditch missionary effort may likely occur.

> 6 And I saw another angel fly in the midst of heaven, having the everlasting gospel to preach unto them that dwell on the earth, and to every nation, and kindred, and tongue, and people,
> 7 Saying with a loud voice, Fear God, and give glory to him; for the hour of his judgment is come: and worship him that made heaven, and earth, and the sea, and the fountains of waters.[4]

What will happen to those individuals who will not take advantage of a last opportunity to accept the gospel of Jesus Christ and join His church?

They will likely experience the wrath of God when it is poured out upon all the world that promotes a Babylonian lifestyle.

> 8 And there followed another angel, saying, Babylon is fallen, is fallen, that great city, because she made all nations drink of the wine of the wrath of her fornication.[5]

Why is the world told not to join with the beast and

---

4. Rev. 14:6-7
5. Rev. 14:8

what are its ramifications?

It appears that this is one of several warnings given to specifically warn the world that the time will come when all must make the decision concerning whether or not to join with the beast by taking upon them his mark. Apparently, there will be no fence sitters. Those who do not take on this mark, could henceforth, experience a martyr's death. However they will be greatly blessed for making the right decision. Those who join with the beast may initially be rewarded by being able to buy and sell, but eventually they will likely suffer death when the wrath of God is poured out. Even then, their decision to join with the beast will torment them, in the afterlife, forever and ever.

> *9 And the third angel followed them, saying with a loud voice, If any man worship the beast and his image, and receive his mark in his forehead, or in his hand,*
> *10 The same shall drink of the wine of the wrath of God, which is poured out without mixture into the cup of his indignation; and he shall be tormented with fire and brimstone in the presence of the holy angels, and in the presence of the Lamb:*
> *11 And the smoke of their torment ascendeth up for ever and ever: and they have no rest day nor night, who worship the beast and his image, and whosoever receiveth the mark of his name.*
> *12 Here is the patience of the saints: here are they that keep the commandments of God, and the faith of Jesus.*
> *13 And I heard a voice from heaven saying unto me, Write, Blessed are the dead which die in the Lord from henceforth: Yea, saith the Spirit, that they may rest from*

their labours; and their works do follow them.[6]

Is the main harvest about to begin?

John was shown a vision that takes place in heaven. He sees Jesus Christ holding a sharp sickle in readiness to initiate the main harvest. Soon the word is given that it is time to reap. On earth, Satan, has the world divided into two camps. Those who have taken on the mark of the beast versus those who have not.[7] The beast will war with the saints and will be successful.[8] Those saints who are overcome but remain faithful to the end will be resurrected to be with Jesus Christ.[9]

> *14 And I looked, and behold a white cloud, and upon the cloud one sat like unto the Son of man, having on his head a golden crown, and in his hand a sharp sickle.*
> *15 And another angel came out of the temple, crying with a loud voice to him that sat on the cloud, Thrust in thy sickle, and reap: for the time is come for thee to reap; for the harvest of the earth is ripe.*
> *16 And he that sat on the cloud thrust in his sickle on the earth; and the earth was reaped.*[10]

What will happen to those who follow the beast?

John saw another angel come out of the temple carrying a sharp sickle. This angel was ordered to reap, by fire, the grapes of the earth which appeared to be the beast, the false prophet and all those who joined with the beast by taking upon them his mark. These individuals will likely experience great torment, which is the great winepress of the wrath of God.

---

6. Rev. 9-13   9. Rev. 15:2
7. Rev. 13:16   10. Rev. 14:14-16
8. Rev. 13:7

17 And another angel came out of the temple which is in heaven, he also having a sharp sickle.

18 And another angel came out from the altar, which had power over fire; and cried with a loud cry to him that had the sharp sickle, saying, Thrust in thy sharp sickle, and gather the clusters of the vine of the earth; for her grapes are fully ripe.

19 And the angel thrust in his sickle into the earth, and gathered the vine of the earth, and cast it into the great winepress of the wrath of God.

20 And the winepress was trodden without the city, and blood came out of the winepress, even unto the horse bridles, by the space of a thousand and six hundred furlongs. [11]

---

11. Rev. 14:17-20

15

Seven Vials

By this time, it appears the only people left on the earth are the followers of the beast and the false prophet, save for a few righteous individuals whom the Lord will protect to either, come forth into the new millennium or be resurrected at the final coming of Jesus Christ.[1]

How will God reap the earth of those who have taken the mark of the beast?

John witnessed the preparations being made in heaven for the wrath of God to be poured out upon the followers of the beast and the false prophet.

> *1 And I saw another sign in heaven, great and marvellous, seven angels having the seven last plagues; for in them is filled up the wrath of God.*[2]

1. Isaiah 24:6
2. Rev. 15:1

How do we know that the saints who did not take on the mark of the beast are in heaven where God resides?

Because John saw them there, he was also informed that these are they who were victorious over the beast and over his mark. And, like the elect, these individuals are allowed to sing the song of the Lamb in joyful worship to the Lord.

> *2 And I saw as it were a sea of glass mingled with fire: and them that had gotten the victory over the beast, and over his image, and over his mark, and over the number of his name, stand on the sea of glass, having the harps of God.*
>
> *3 And they sing the song of Moses the servant of God, and the song of the Lamb, saying, Great and marvellous are thy works, Lord God Almighty; just and true are thy ways, thou King of saints.*
>
> *4 Who shall not fear thee, O Lord, and glorify thy name? For thou only art holy: for all nations shall come and worship before thee; for thy judgments are made manifest.[3]*

How will the wrath of God be initiated?

John saw the temple doors open and seven angels appear. These seven angels each will receive a vial of wrath, which, when poured out will cause great destruction on the earth. Following this, the doors of the temple were shut. This action may indicate that, from henceforth, no one will be resurrected into

---

3. Rev. 15:2-4

heaven until all the vials of wrath have been poured out and the destruction is done.

5 And after that I looked, and, behold, the temple of the tabernacle of the testimony in heaven was opened:

6 And the seven angels came out of the temple, having the seven plagues, clothed in pure and white linen, and having their breasts girded with golden girdles.

7 And one of the four beasts gave unto the seven angels seven golden vials full of the wrath of God, who liveth for ever and ever.

8 And the temple was filled with smoke from the glory of God, and from his power; and no man was able to enter into the temple, till the seven plagues of the seven angels were fulfilled.[4]

---

4. Rev. 15:5-8

16

Judgment Begins

At this point, having overcome most of the righteous saints, the beast and the false prophet may think they are in complete control of the world. Approximately 42 months may have past since the sound of the seventh trumpet.[1]

How is the order given to pour out the vials of wrath upon the earth?

John witnessed the giving of the final word that will initiate the destruction of the wicked. As the angel said, "the time has arrived to destroy those who destroy the earth." [2] And since man has destroyed the earth, it appears that God will now destroy all mankind who have worshipped the beast.

1 And I heard a great voice out of the temple saying to

---

1. Rev. 13:5
2. Rev. 11:18

*the seven angels, Go your ways, and pour out the vials of
the wrath of God upon the earth.[3]*

What happened when the first vial was poured out?

There fell an offensive and grievous sore upon the men who
had worshipped the beast by taking on his mark. This is very
similar to the plague of boils that Moses used to afflict the
Egyptians. Moses was asked to take a handful of ash from the
furnace and throw it into the air. This caused the Egyptians to
writh in pain from festering boils.[4]

> *2 And the first went, and poured out his vial upon the
> earth; and there fell a noisome and grievous sore upon
> the men which had the mark of the beast, and upon them
> which worshipped his image.[5]*

When the second vial is poured what will happen?

The sea became as blood and every soul will die in the sea.
Again, this is similar to when God told Moses to stretch out his
hand over the waters of Egypt and all the waters were turned to
blood.[6]

> *3 And the second angel poured out his vial upon the sea;
> and it became as the blood of a dead man: and every
> living soul died in the sea.[7]*

What will happen when the angel pours the third vial upon the earth?

---

3. Rev. 16:1   6. Ex. 7:19-20
4. Ex. 9:10-11   7. Rev. 16:3
5. Rev. 16:2

John saw that all the rivers and fountains will turn to blood.

> *4 And the third angel poured out his vial upon the rivers*
> *and fountains of waters; and they became blood.*[8]

Why will God turn the waters of the earth to blood?

John was told it is because the beast and his followers will shed the blood of the saints and prophets. Thus God will be justified in giving them blood to drink.

> *5 And I heard the angel of the waters say, Thou art*
> *righteous, O Lord, which art, and wast, and shalt be,*
> *because thou hast judged thus.*
> *6 For they have shed the blood of saints and prophets,*
> *and thou hast given them blood to drink; for they are*
> *worthy.*
> *7 And I heard another out of the altar say, Even so, Lord*
> *God Almighty, true and righteous are thy judgments.*[9]

Since man may have destroyed much of the atmosphere by using nuclear weapons; how will the Lord use the heavenly elements to torment man?

John saw that the sun will be used to scorch man with fire. Moses used another heavenly element to torment the Egyptians. He was told to stretch forth his hand over Egypt and three days of darkness would cover the land.[10]

> *8 And the fourth angel poured out his vial upon the sun;*

---

8. Rev. 16:4
9. Rev. 16:5-7
10. Ex. 10:21-22

and power was given unto him to scorch men with fire.
9 And men were scorched with great heat, and
blasphemed the name of God, which hath power over
these plagues: and they repented not to give him glory.[11]

What happened as the fifth angel poured out his vial?

When the fifth vial is poured out the beast and his followers
will personally feel the pain of their deeds because this will be
poured directly upon his seat of government. Still they will not
repent.

10 And the fifth angel poured out his vial upon the seat
of the beast; and his kingdom was full of darkness; and
they gnawed their tongues for pain,
11 And blasphemed the God of heaven because of their
pains and their sores, and repented not of their deeds.[12]

What will the sixth vial cause to happen?

The pouring of this vial will prepare the armies of the world
to be destroyed in one place. John is shown that the beast and
the false prophet will send out emissaries to the kings of the
world to gather them to battle.

12 And the sixth angel poured out his vial upon the great
river Euphrates; and the water thereof was dried up, that
the way of the kings of the east might be prepared.
13 And I saw three unclean spirits like frogs come out of
the mouth of the dragon, and out of the mouth of the beast,
and out of the mouth of the false prophet.

---

11. Rev. 16:8-9
12. Rev. 16:10-11

> *14 For they are the spirits of devils, working miracles,*
> *which go forth unto the kings of the earth and of the whole*
> *world, to gather them to the battle of that great day of*
> *God Almighty.*[13]

Will there be one last warning?

One last warning will be given by the Lord. Behold I come
as a thief. To the beast and his followers this warning will likely
fall on deaf ears. Truly the final coming of the Lord will be as
a thief, because the beast and his followers will be blind in
their ability to interpret the scriptures—as indicated by their
lack of repentance.

> *15 Behold, I come as a thief. Blessed is he that watcheth,*
> *and keepeth his garments, lest he walk naked, and they*
> *see his shame.*[14]

Where will this great final battle be fought?

North of Jerusalem lies a great valley called Miggido, another ancient name for it is Armageddo or Armageddon. This
is where the Lord will gather the armies of the world.

> *16 And he gathered them together into a place called in*
> *the Hebrew tongue Armageddon.*[15]

When the seventh angel pours out his vial what will happen?

---

13. Rev. 16:12-14
14. Rev. 16:15
15. Rev. 16:16

God will declare it is done. Possibly, meaning the last series of events will begin. First, a great earthquake will occur—the greatest earthquake known to man. Secondly, the great city will be divided into three parts. Third, the cities of the nations will fall. Fourth, the great Babylon will come into remembrance before God, to receive the fierceness of His wrath. Fifth, islands will flee and mountains will be made low. And finally, a great plague of hail will fall upon men during the time of Armageddon.

> *17 And the seventh angel poured out his vial into the air; and there came a great voice out of the temple of heaven, from the throne, saying, It is done.*
>
> *18 And there were voices, and thunders, and lightnings; and there was a great earthquake, such as was not since men were upon the earth, so mighty an earthquake, and so great.*
>
> *19 And the great city was divided into three parts, and the cities of the nations fell: and great Babylon came in remembrance before God, to give unto her the cup of the wine of the fierceness of his wrath.*
>
> *20 And every island fled away, and the mountains were not found.*
>
> *21 And there fell upon men a great hail out of heaven, every stone about the weight of a talent: and men blasphemed God because of the plague of the hail; for the plague thereof was exceeding great.*[16]

---

16. Rev. 16:17-21

17

Babylon, Beast & Ten Kings

J ohn was suddenly presented with another historical
background sketch concerning who Babylon really is,
the role she plays and how she interacts with Satan,
the beast and the ten kings.

What did the angel say to John concerning the judgment of the great whore?

John was told he will witness her judgment.

> *1 And there came one of the seven angels which had the seven vials, and talked with me, saying unto me, Come hither; I will shew unto thee the judgment of the great whore that sitteth upon many waters:*
> *2 With whom the kings of the earth have committed*

fornication, and the inhabitants of the earth have been made drunk with the wine of her fornication.[1]

Who is Babylon?

In premortal life, Satan had been cast out of heaven for in-surrection.[2] When he was cast to earth, he brought with him a third of the angels of heaven.[3] With the help of these and other spirits, born on earth over time, Satan has been able to put together an efficient organization. It appears that the goal of this organization is to enable Satan to be the supreme ruler of this world. To remain in power, it seems, there is nothing he will not do. To him, the end always justifies the means. People exist only to be used as commodities to help him remain in control. To accomplish this, he has organized a very efficient government. His leaders have been hand picked, because they embrace the same lust for power and the same philosophy of living. The tools they use to stay in power include killing, ly-ing, cheating, fornication, adultery, prostitution, bribery, steal-ing, greed, blasphemy, blackmail, revenge, and coercion. The rewards Satan uses to facilitate his goals are fame, fortune, status, glory, power, and idol worship. The Lord refers to this organization as Babylon or, the Church of Satan. The term Babylon was probably selected because this ancient city epito-mized the philosophy of this organization. Later, we find John comparing this organization to Rome. The term Babylon, is not tied to a single city, but it used to represent any organiza-tion that functions by using the same philosophy and tools mentioned above. As a symbol the Lord refers to Babylon as a woman. Possibly, because a woman has the ability to appear

1. Rev. 17:1-2
2. Ezek. 28:13-15; Rev. 12:3,5
3. Rev. 12:4, 7-9

beautiful, innocent, provocative, enticing, yet, can be very devious. John now sees the woman sitting upon seven mountains or possibly continents. The seven heads still represent the seven world leaders (of which six are dead).[4] And the ten horns still represent the ten leaders, who in the last days will support the beast.[5]

> 3 So he carried me away in the spirit into the wilderness: and I saw a woman sit upon a scarlet coloured beast, full of names of blasphemy, having seven heads and ten horns.[6]

What is the meaning of the cup of abominations that the woman is holding in her hand?

The purple and scarlet seem to represent political power. The gold, precious stones, and pearls appear to represent wealth, fame, and pride. The golden cup filled with abominations and filthiness of her fornications could all be symbolic of what she had to do to achieve this fame, wealth, and political power.

> 4 And the woman was arrayed in purple and scarlet colour, and decked with gold and precious stones and pearls, having a golden cup in her hand full of abominations and filthiness of her fornication:[7]

What is the meaning of MYSTERY and MOTHER OF HARLOTS?

As a mystery, she appears to represent herself as one thing

---

4. Rev. 17:9, 10   7. Rev. 17:4
5. Rev. 17:12
6. Rev. 17:3

but is completely the opposite, this is how she seduces. As Babylon the Great, she seems to represent the ultimate in pride, wealth, and political power. As a mother can bring life into existence, a mother of harlots and abominations can bring evil into existence.

> 5 And upon her forehead was a name written, MYSTERY, BABYLON THE GREAT, THE MOTHER OF HARLOTS AND ABOMINATIONS OF THE EARTH. [8]

Why was John astonished at the sight of this woman?

He was likely amazed to see how this woman will use her political power to bring to pass the martyrdom of the saints of Jesus Christ.

> 6 And I saw the woman drunken with the blood of the saints, and with the blood of the martyrs of Jesus: and when I saw her, I wondered with great admiration. [9]

How can this woman bring to pass the martyrdom of the saints?

To help John understand, the angel explained the mystery of the woman, the beast, the seven heads, and the ten horns.

> 7 And the angel said unto me, Wherefore didst thou marvel? I will tell thee the mystery of the woman, and of the beast that carrieth her, which hath the seven heads and ten horns. [10]

---

8. Rev. 17:5
9. Rev. 17:6
10. Rev. 17:7

Again, who is the beast that was, is not, and yet is?

As explained previously, the head of the beast is probably the leader that will come to power in the last days. It is possible that he could be elected to an office over that great nation that has the power to destroy like a leopard, bear, and lion. Eventually, he could serve out his term of office. Later he could run for this office again and be elected. This is how the saying, "was, and is not, and yet is, may be fulfilled. In other words, he was the leader, is not the leader, and yet is the leader again.

> 8 *The beast that thou sawest was, and is not; and shall ascend out of the bottomless pit, and go into perdition: and they that dwell on the earth shall wonder, whose names were not written in the book of life from the foundation of the world, when they behold the beast that was, and is not, and yet is.*[11]

Again, what are the seven heads of the beast?

The seven heads may represent seven mountains, (possibly seven continents, thus indicating a worldwide presence) on which the woman sitteth. The seven heads also represent seven kings, five are dead, one is currently living in John's time) And the other is not yet come. When he does come (in the last days), he will continue in power for a short time.

> 9 *And here is the mind which hath wisdom. The seven heads are seven mountains, on which the woman sitteth.*

---

11. Rev. 17:8

> *10 And there are seven kings: five are fallen, and one is, and the other is not yet come; and when he cometh, he must continue a short space.*[12]

Again, how can the beast that was and is not be the eighth, yet still be of the seven?

As explained previously, it is possible that in the last days, an individual could be elected to office the first time, thus he would become the seventh beast. After his term of office runs out, he could step down for a while and then run for office again and be reelected. Thus he could fulfill prophecy by becoming the eighth world leader, but is still one of the original seven.

> *11 And the beast that was, and is not, even he is the eighth, and is of the seven, and goeth into perdition.*[13]

Again, what do the ten horns represent?

The ten horns represent ten kings who will rise to power in the last days. And will use this power to support the beast for one hour, or the 42 months that the beast will continue in power.[14]

> *12 And the ten horns which thou sawest are ten kings, which have received no kingdom as yet; but receive power as kings one hour with the beast.*
> *13 These have one mind, and shall give their power and strength unto the beast.*[15]

---

12. Rev. 17:9-10   15. Rev. 17:12-13
13. Rev. 17:11
14. Rev. 13:5

How will these ten kings support the beast?

It appears, they will pool their efforts to make war with Jesus Christ. But they will not prevail.

> *14 These shall make war with the Lamb, and the Lamb shall overcome them: for he is Lord of lords, and King of kings: and they that are with him are called, and chosen, and faithful.*[16]

What are the waters where the whore sitteth which John saw?

The waters are the people, multitudes, and nations of the world.

> *15 And he saith unto me, The waters which thou sawest, where the whore sitteth, are peoples, and multitudes, and nations, and tongues.*[17]

What will the ten kings do to the whore?

They shall destroy Babylon with fire. Thus proving there is no honor among thieves.

> *16 And the ten horns which thou sawest upon the beast, these shall hate the whore, and shall make her desolate and naked, and shall eat her flesh, and burn her with fire.*[18]

---

16. Rev. 17:14
17. Rev. 17:15
18. Rev. 17:16

Why will these ten kings be willing to support the beast?

Because God will put it in their hearts to fulfill his will. So that His words will be fulfilled.

> 17 For God hath put in their hearts to fulfil his will, and
> to agree, and give their kingdom unto the beast, until the
> words of God shall be fulfilled.[19]

What great city represents Babylon?

Rome was the great city in John's time that most likely served as the symbol of Babylon. However, it appears that this name was simply used as a symbol to represent all great cities in our time. Thus when we speak of Babylon in our day it means all great cities of the world.

> 18 And the woman which thou sawest is that great city,
> which reigneth over the kings of the earth.[20]

---

19. Rev. 17:17
20. Rev. 17:18

18

Fall of Babylon

n angel explained to John why the destruction of Babylon is justified.

Why is the destruction of Babylon necessary?

Apparently, it is because she had participated with the leaders and merchants of the world in subverting righteousness and promoting evil and wickedness.

> *1 And after these things I saw another angel come down from heaven, having great power; and the earth was lightened with his glory.*
> *2 And he cried mightily with a strong voice, saying, Babylon the great is fallen, is fallen, and is become the habitation of devils, and the hold of every foul spirit, and a cage of every unclean and hateful bird.*
> *3 For all nations have drunk of the wine of the wrath of her fornication, and the kings of the earth have committed*

fornication with her, and the merchants of the earth are
waxed rich through the abundance of her delicacies.[1]

What must happen before the destruction can begin?

John heard a voice from heaven warning the saints to come
out of Babylon. Again, Babylon seems to represent all large
cities of the world. Therefore, this warning is for all saints who
may be living in these cities.

> *4 And I heard another voice from heaven, saying, Come*
> *out of her, my people, that ye be not partakers of her sins,*
> *and that ye receive not of her plagues.[2]*

How terrible will be the destruction of Babylon?

The angel reminded John that God is aware of all the wickedness of Babylon and, not only, will he reward her, as she
rewarded the saints, but He will double that reward. When the
destruction occurs Babylon will be in a state of shock because
she thinks she is so great that nothing can ever happen to her.

> *5 For her sins have reached unto heaven, and God hath*
> *remembered her iniquities.*
> *6 Reward her even as she rewarded you, and double unto*
> *her double according to her works: in the cup which she*
> *hath filled fill to her double.*
> *7 How much she hath glorified herself, and lived*
> *deliciously, so much torment and sorrow give her: for*
> *she saith in her heart, I sit a queen, and am no widow,*
> *and shall see no sorrow.[3]*

---

1. Rev. 18:1-3
2. Rev. 18:4
3. Rev. 18:5-7

How quickly will Babylon be destroyed?

John is told her destruction will come in one day and she will be burned by fire.

> *8 Therefore shall her plagues come in one day, death, and mourning, and famine; and she shall be utterly burned with fire: for strong is the Lord God who judgeth her.[4]*

How will the various world leaders react to the destruction of Babylon?

John was shown that the kings of the earth who have joined with Babylon in persecuting the saints and promoting evil will mourn for her as they see the smoke of her destruction billowing skyward.

> *9 And the kings of the earth, who have committed fornication and lived deliciously with her, shall bewail her, and lament for her, when they shall see the smoke of her burning,*
> *10 Standing afar off for the fear of her torment, saying, Alas, alas, that great city Babylon, that mighty city! For in one hour is thy judgment come.[5]*

Why will the merchants of the earth mourn for her?

It seems, the reason the merchants are mourning, is not for the love of the city, but because of greed. In other words, who

---

4. Rev. 18:8
5. Rev. 18:9-10

will now buy their merchandise?

> *11 And the merchants of the earth shall weep and mourn*
> *over her; for no man buyeth their merchandise any more:*
> *12 The merchandise of gold, and silver, and precious*
> *stones, and of pearls, and fine linen, and purple, and*
> *silk, and scarlet, and all thine wood, and all manner*
> *vessels of ivory, and all manner vessels of most precious*
> *wood, and of brass, and iron, and marble,*
> *13 And cinnamon, and odours, and ointments, and*
> *frankincense, and wine, and oil, and fine flour, and wheat,*
> *and beasts, and sheep, and horses, and chariots, and*
> *slaves, and souls of men.*
> *14 And the fruits that thy soul lusted after are departed*
> *from thee, and all things which were dainty and goodly*
> *are departed from thee, and thou shalt find them no more*
> *at all.*
> *15 The merchants of these things, which were made rich*
> *by her, shall stand afar off for the fear of her torment,*
> *weeping and wailing,*
> *16 And saying, Alas, alas, that great city, that was clothed*
> *in fine linen, and purple, and scarlet, and decked with*
> *gold, and precious stones, and pearls!* [6]

Why are the shipmasters and sailors mourning?

John saw that it was for the same reason as the merchants. It
was simple greed. For they are probably thinking, how are we
going to live? What will happen to us?

> *17 For in one hour so great riches is come to nought.*
> *And every shipmaster, and all the company in ships, and*

---

6. Rev. 18:11-16

sailors, and as many as trade by sea, stood afar off,
18 And cried when they saw the smoke of her burning,
saying, What city is like unto this great city!
19 And they cast dust on their heads, and cried, weeping
and wailing, saying, Alas, alas, that great city, wherein
were made rich all that had ships in the sea by reason of
her costliness! For in one hour is she made desolate.[7]

Why is heaven rejoicing over the fall of Babylon?

Because Babylon was deeply involved in the slaying of the saints and prophets. It is for this reason, that God's vengeance is such that Babylon will be thrown down, then burned, to rise no more.

20 Rejoice over her, thou heaven, and ye holy apostles
and prophets; for God hath avenged you on her.
21 And a mighty angel took up a stone like a great
millstone, and cast it into the sea, saying, Thus with
violence shall that great city Babylon be thrown down,
and shall be found no more at all.
22 And the voice of harpers, and musicians, and of pipers,
and trumpeters, shall be heard no more at all in thee;
and no craftsman, of whatsoever craft he be, shall be
found any more in thee; and the sound of a millstone
shall be heard no more at all in thee;
23 And the light of a candle shall shine no more at all in
thee; and the voice of the bridegroom and of the bride
shall be heard no more at all in thee: for thy merchants
were the great men of the earth; for by thy sorceries were
all nations deceived.
24 And in her was found the blood of prophets, and of
saints, and of all that were slain upon the earth.[8]

---

7. Rev. 18:17-19
8. Rev. 18:20-24

19

Wedding, Marriage Supper & the Final Coming

After Babylon is destroyed, the armies of the world will converge together at Armageddon to fight the greatest battle in the history of the world. It will be a battle between the forces of evil and the forces of righteousness led by Jesus Christ.

Why is there joy in heaven?

John sees the twenty four elders, four beasts, and multitudes of saints rejoicing and expressing their thankfulness by worshipping God for being allowed to participate in a sacred heavenly event.

1 And after these things I heard a great voice of much people in heaven, saying, Alleluia; Salvation, and glory, and honour, and power, unto the Lord our God:

2 For true and righteous are his judgments: for he hath judged the great whore, which did corrupt the earth with her fornication, and hath avenged the blood of his servants at her hand.

3 And again they said, Alleluia. And her smoke rose up for ever and ever.

4 And the four and twenty elders and the four beasts fell down and worshipped God that sat on the throne, saying, Amen; Alleluia.

5 And a voice came out of the throne, saying, Praise our God, all ye his servants, and ye that fear him, both small and great.

6 And I heard as it were the voice of a great multitude, and as the voice of many waters, and as the voice of mighty thunderings, saying, Alleluia: for the Lord God omnipotent reigneth.[1]

What sacred event is about to happen in heaven?

John saw that the bride (the Church) is now ready. That the time for the marriage to the Lamb (Jesus Christ) has come. This is the moment (in heaven) when all righteous members of the Church of Jesus Christ will become one with the Savior, as a bride is one with her husband. To become joint heirs of all the blessings that God the Father has in store for His Son and His bride.

7 Let us be glad and rejoice, and give honour to him: for the marriage of the Lamb is come, and his wife hath made herself ready.[2]

1. Rev. 19:1-6
2. Rev. 19:7

What does the fine white linen represent?

It symbolizes the righteousness of the saints.

> *8 And to her was granted that she should be arrayed in fine linen, clean and white: for the fine linen is the righteousness of saints.[3]*

What was John told to write concerning the marriage feast?

A standard Hebrew wedding (of that day) will consummate the marriage and then celebrate with a wedding feast. Since it appears that the wedding has already taken place, John was told to write, blessed are they which are called unto the marriage supper of the Lamb. This is to emphasize how important it is to be called into that marriage supper. Also to know that it is only the very righteous, those who have lived the commandments of Jesus Christ and those who have a testimony of His name. Thus it seems this wedding feast also occurs in heaven.

> *9 And he saith unto me, Write, Blessed are they which are called unto the marriage supper of the Lamb. And he saith unto me, These are the true sayings of God.*
> *10 And I fell at his feet to worship him. And he said unto me, See thou do it not: I am thy fellowservant, and of thy brethren that have the testimony of Jesus: worship God: for the testimony of Jesus is the spirit of prophecy.[4]*

What is THE event that all mankind has been waiting

---

3. Rev. 19:8
4. Rev. 19:9-10

for since the days of Adam and Eve?

John witnessed the final coming of Jesus Christ. He saw Jesus Christ on a white horse and described the Savior in His glorified body. It seems, that the Savior was dressed in apparel dipped in blood, possibly to symbolize the blood of the martyrd saints as justification to make war.

> *11 And I saw heaven opened, and behold a white horse; and he that sat upon him was called Faithful and True, and in righteousness he doth judge and make war.*
> *12 His eyes were as a flame of fire, and on his head were many crowns; and he had a name written, that no man knew, but he himself.*
> *13 And he was clothed with a vesture dipped in blood: and his name is called The Word of God.[5]*

Who did John see riding behind the Savior?

He saw heavenly armies, which are the saints of Jesus Christ, dressed in white linen and riding upon white horses.

> *14 And the armies which were in heaven followed him upon white horses, clothed in fine linen, white and clean.[6]*

How will Christ govern?

John was told that the word of Jesus will be like a two-edged sword. That with it, He will rule the nations. That His word will be like a rod of iron. This indicates that the Savior

---

5. Rev. 19:11-13
6. Rev. 19:14

will set up a government that will be the Kingdom of God on earth. And this government will rule by the word of Jesus Christ.

> *15 And out of his mouth goeth a sharp sword, that with it he should smite the nations: and he shall rule them with a rod of iron: and he treadeth the winepress of the fierceness and wrath of Almighty God.*
> *16 And he hath on his vesture and on his thigh a name written, KING OF KINGS, AND LORD OF LORDS.[7]*

What will happen when Christ arrives at Armageddon?

A horrendous battle ensues with Christ emerging victoriously. John describes the slaughter of the armies of Satan as being so great that he saw an angel calling to the fowls of the air to come and partake of the flesh of kings, captains, mighty men and horses.

> *17 And I saw an angel standing in the sun; and he cried with a loud voice, saying to all the fowls that fly in the midst of heaven, Come and gather yourselves together unto the supper of the great God;*
> *18 That ye may eat the flesh of kings, and the flesh of captains, and the flesh of mighty men, and the flesh of horses, and of them that sit on them, and the flesh of all men, both free and bond, both small and great.[8]*

What will happen to the beast and the false prophet?

John saw that the beast and the false prophet will be taken

---

7. Rev. 19:15-16
8. Rev. 19:17-18

and cast alive into a place where their punishment is compared
to being confined in a lake of fire burning with sulfur.

> *19 And I saw the beast, and the kings of the earth, and
> their armies, gathered together to make war against him
> that sat on the horse, and against his army.*
> *20 And the beast was taken, and with him the false
> prophet that wrought miracles before him, with which he
> deceived them that had received the mark of the beast,
> and them that worshipped his image. These both were
> cast alive into a lake of fire burning with brimstone.*[9]

What will happen to the rest of the armies of Satan?

The rest will be slain by word of the Savior and the fowls
will be filled with their flesh.

> *21 And the remnant were slain with the sword of him
> that sat upon the horse, which sword proceeded out of
> his mouth: and all the fowls were filled with their flesh.*[10]

---

9. Rev. 19:19-20
10. Rev. 19:21

20

Disposition of Satan & the Wicked

J esus Christ has arrived from heaven, Armageddon has been fought and Satan has lost. The beast and false prophet have been captured and thrown into a place where their soul will be tormented forever and ever.

But what about Satan? What will happen to him?

John saw an angel descend from heaven. This angel was holding a chain and the key to the bottomless pit. Satan is captured by this angel, bound with a chain and shut away in the pit for one thousand years. During this time he will be able to deceive no one. After this thousand year period expires Satan will be loosed for a short time.

1 And I saw an angel come down from heaven, having

the key of the bottomless pit and a great chain in his hand.
2 And he laid hold on the dragon, that old serpent, which
is the Devil, and Satan, and bound him a thousand years,
3 And cast him into the bottomless pit, and shut him up,
and set a seal upon him, that he should deceive the nations
no more, till the thousand years should be fulfilled: and
after that he must be loosed a little season.[1]

What will happen to the followers of Jesus Christ who were most obedient in obeying His teachings and were willing to be separated from society by not taking on the mark of the beast?

John saw that they were given thrones and the privilege to live and rule with the Lord for a thousand years. As mentioned previously, most of the saints will have been martyrd. Apparently there will also be a few that were not killed but somehow survived after being cut off from society.[2] These saints were able to maintain a faithful testimony by remaining obedient to the commandments of Jesus. And, most importantly, they did not take on the mark of the beast. It seems that some of these individuals will be resurrected at that final coming of Jesus Christ. Thus they appear to be the gleanings of the harvest and some will stay on Earth to become the first progenitors of the new millennium.

4 And I saw thrones, and they sat upon them, and
judgment was given unto them: and I saw the souls of
them that were beheaded for the witness of Jesus, and for
the word of God, and which had not worshipped the beast,
neither his image, neither had received his mark upon

1. Rev. 20:1-3
2. Isaiah 24:6

their foreheads, or in their hands; and they lived and reigned with Christ a thousand years.[3]

What will happen to the rest of the dead?

John was told that the rest of the dead would not be resurrected for a thousand years. This appears to be known as, "the second resurrection". A careful reading seems to indicate that the statement, "This is the first resurrection". Listed below, is a reference to the saints who lived with Christ for one thousand years.[4]

> *5 But the rest of the dead lived not again until the thousand years were finished. This is the first resurrection.[5]*

What is the meaning of the second death?

In this context, the second death seems to refer to a type of spiritual death. In other words, the spirit is cut off from any person, place, or thing, that involves holiness or righteousness. Thus those who come forth in the first resurrection will not take part in this second death. While those who are cast into the lake of fire and brimstone, such as the beast and false prophet, will continue to experience this second death forever and ever.

> *6 Blessed and holy is he that hath part in the first resurrection: on such the second death hath no power, but they shall be priests of God and of Christ, and shall*

---

3. Rev. 20:4
4. Rev. 20:4
5. Rev. 20:5

reign with him a thousand years.[6]

What will happen after this thousand year period is over?

Satan will be released from his prison to, again, deceive and tempt mankind. Eventually, wickedness will permeate the world. Thus John sees a repetition of history. Again, the armies of Satan will unite to battle the Lord. As this army prepares to annihilate the saints, fire will come down from heaven and destroy all his armies, only the saints will be left alive.

> *7 And when the thousand years are expired, Satan shall be loosed out of his prison,*
> *8 And shall go out to deceive the nations which are in the four quarters of the earth, Gog and Magog, to gather them together to battle: the number of whom is as the sand of the sea.*
> *9 And they went up on the breadth of the earth, and compassed the camp of the saints about, and the beloved city: and fire came down from God out of heaven, and devoured them.*[7]

What will happen to Satan?

John was told that Satan will join the beast and the false prophet by being cast into the lake of fire and brimstone where they will be tormented day and night forever.

> *10 And the devil that deceived them was cast into the lake of fire and brimstone, where the beast and the false*

---

6. Rev. 20:6
7. Rev. 20:7-9

prophet are, and shall be tormented day and night for ever and ever.[8]

Will Satan, the beast, and the false prophet, ever be able to return to where God the Father and Jesus Christ reside?

John was told that where God the Father reigns there will never be any place for them.

> *11 And I saw a great white throne, and him that sat on it, from whose face the earth and the heaven fled away; and there was found no place for them.*[9]

For those who have waited a thousand years in hell, how will they be judged?

As these individuals stand before God the books will be opened and they will be judged out of these books. In accordance with their works on earth. Those who have accomplished much will receive much, while those who have accomplished little will receive little. After the last person is released from hell, then death and hell will only exist for Satan and his co-conspirators who will continue to experience the second (spiritual) death.

> *12 And I saw the dead, small and great, stand before God; and the books were opened: and another book was opened, which is the book of life: and the dead were judged out of those things which were written in the books,*

---

8. Rev. 20:10
9. Rev. 20:11

according to their works.

13 And the sea gave up the dead which were in it; and death and hell delivered up the dead which were in them: and they were judged every man according to their works.

14 And death and hell were cast into the lake of fire. This is the second death.

15 And whosoever was not found written in the book of life was cast into the lake of fire. [10]

---

10. Rev. 20:12-15

21

Holy City

The final judgment is now completed. Each earthly participant has stood at the judgement bar of God. Some having heard the words, "Depart from me, ye that work iniquity".[1] while others hear, "Come, ye blessed of my Father, inherit the kingdom prepared for you from the foundation of the world:"[2]

What will happen to our current heaven and earth?

John saw that our current heaven and earth will be dissolved and a new earth and a new heaven created.

> *1 And I saw a new heaven and a new earth: for the first heaven and the first earth were passed away; and there was no more sea.[3]*

---

1. Matt. 7:23
2. Matt 25:34
3. Rev. 21:1

What was seen coming down from heaven?

John saw the descent of a glorious holy city, called the new Jerusalem. This city is so beautiful that John said, it was prepared as a bride adorned for her husband.

> *2 And I John saw the holy city, new Jerusalem, coming down from God out of heaven, prepared as a bride adorned for her husband.[4]*

Who will dwell in this city?

A voice from heaven declared to John that God will dwell with His people in this holy city.

> *3 And I heard a great voice out of heaven saying, Behold, the tabernacle of God is with men, and he will dwell with them, and they shall be his people, and God himself shall be with them, and be their God.[5]*

Will pain and sorrow exist any more for the inhabitants of this city?

John was told that death, sorrow, crying and pain will no longer be experienced. That unhappiness was a part of our former earth life and that earth exists no more.

> *4 And God shall wipe away all tears from their eyes; and there shall be no more death, neither sorrow, nor crying, neither shall there be any more pain: for the former things are passed away. [6]*

---

4. Rev. 21:2
5. Rev. 21:3
6. Rev. 21:4

What else does God promise to those that are allowed to inhabit this city?

Permission will be given by the Lord to drink from the fountain of the waters of life. In other words, it appears the inhabitants of this city will be blessed with eternal life.

> *5 And he that sat upon the throne said, Behold, I make all things new. And he said unto me, Write: for these words are true and faithful.*
> *6 And he said unto me, It is done. I am Alpha and Omega, the beginning and the end. I will give unto him that is athirst of the fountain of the water of life freely.[7]*

What else does the Lord promise to His people?

Since they have overcome the trials and tribulations of earth life, John now understands that they shall become co-inheritors with Jesus Christ. In other words, He will be their God and they will be His son.

> *7 He that overcometh shall inherit all things; and I will be his God, and he shall be my son.[8]*

Will any unrighteous people (from our former earth) be allowed into this city?

John was told that none of the previous earth's unrighteous inhabitants will be allowed into this holy place. All Satan and his leaders can expect to receive is their part in the second/

---

7. Rev. 21:5-6
8. Rev. 21:7

spiritual death.

> 8 But the fearful, and unbelieving, and the abominable,
> and murderers, and whoremongers, and sorcerers, and
> idolaters, and all liars, shall have their part in the lake
> which burneth with fire and brimstone: which is the
> second death.[9]

John was shown, the elaborate and exquisite construction that was incorporated into the building of this holy city. Why does the angel refer to this city as the wife of Jesus Christ?

As previously mentioned, in premortal life, Satan had been cast out of heaven[10] for insurrection.[11] When he was cast to earth he brought with him a third of the angels in heaven.[12] It appears that with the help of these and other spirits, born on earth over time, Satan has been able to put together a very efficient organization. To counter this, it appears that the Savior has been able to set up His church.[13] The goal of this church was to help the saints achieve eternal life by forsaking sin.[14] Unfortunately, when the Savior tried to set up this church on earth, He was killed and His church was removed into the wilderness to be protected from Satan.[15] Later, it was restored from this wilderness.[16] The leaders appear to be handpicked, by the Savior, because they embrace His same philosophy for living. The tools they appear to use include: love, service to others, righteous thoughts, fellowshipping, setting the right example, honesty, truthfulness and concern for others. The rewards seem

---

9. Rev. 21:8
10. Ezek. 28:13-15
11. Rev. 12:3,7-9
12. Rev. 12:4, 7-9
13. Eph. 5:23
14. Rom. 6:22-23
15. Rev. 12:6
16. Rev. 12:13

to include: a good feeling, magnification of character attributes, and the development of lasting ties to family and friends. However, (as John was told concerning the seven churches) most of the Lord's rewards are reserved for an afterlife and are given to those who endure to the end.

As a symbol, the Lord refers to His church as a woman,[17] possibly because the woman has the ability to be: loving, protective, caring, nurturing, long suffering, and very spiritual. Now that earth life has passed away, the Church of Jesus Christ seems to be represented by an actual city, called the holy/new Jerusalem. It is designed to house the inhabitants that lived the gospel and overcame sin. John had the opportunity to see the Lamb's wife (the holy Jerusalem) descend out of the heaven from God.

> 9 And there came unto me one of the seven angels which had the seven vials full of the seven last plagues, and talked with me, saying, Come hither, I will shew thee the bride, the Lamb's wife.
>
> 10 And he carried me away in the spirit to a great and high mountain, and shewed me that great city, the holy Jerusalem, descending out of heaven from God,[18]

What is the glory of God?

The glory of God is apparently a brilliant light that some have compared in brightness to a type of lightening. John was shown that this city emits a clear light, as if being projected through precious stones. This light seems to be similar to the glorious light that is projected by God.

---

17. Rev. 21:9
18. Rev. 21:9-10

11 Having the glory of God: and her light was like unto
a stone most precious, even like a jasper stone, clear as
crystal;[19]

What do the twelve gates and the twelve angels represent?

An angel explained to John that the twelve gates represent
the twelve tribes of Israel. Possibly indicating that all who enter this city can trace their lineage, or adopted lineage, back to
one of the twelve tribes of Israel.[20] The angel guarding each
gate stands as a sentinel to ensure that no one enters this city
unworthily.

12 And had a wall great and high, and had twelve gates,
and at the gates twelve angels, and names written thereon,
which are the names of the twelve tribes of the children
of Israel:
13 On the east three gates; on the north three gates; on
the south three gates; and on the west three gates.[21]

What does the foundation of the wall surrounding the city represent?

John saw that this city wall was built on twelve great foundations. Thus, the foundation of this wall will last forever. Im-
bedded in each foundation was found the name of an apostle
of Jesus Christ, possibly suggesting that this wall was symbolically built on the foundation of apostles and prophets.

19. Rev. 21:11
20. Gen. 17:1-6, 22:15-18
21. Rev. 21:12-13

14 And the wall of the city had twelve foundations, and in them the names of the twelve apostles of the Lamb.[22]

Why did the angel measure the city and the walls of the city?

The angel wanted John to know that this city was approximately 1400 miles wide and 1400 miles long. In other words, it was square. Possibly, the squareness of this city represents perfection in character attributes. All qualities that characterize the individuals that live therein. The walls were measured to show John how enormous they were (approximately 2,160 feet high). These great walls seem to indicate this city will be protected against all enemies for the eternities. Also the hundred and forty four cubits may be used to symbolically honor the 144,000 missionary force. How can a hundred and forty four cubits be compared to 144,000 missionaries? When a church is small it is vulnerable to being destroyed. As a missionary force builds up a church it becomes strong and less susceptible to destruction. Thus as a wall protects a city, a large church built by a strong missionary force can protect its members.

15 And he that talked with me had a golden reed to measure the city, and the gates thereof, and the wall thereof.
16 And the city lieth foursquare, and the length is as large as the breadth: and he measured the city with the reed, twelve thousand furlongs. The length and the breadth and the height of it are equal.
17 And he measured the wall thereof, an hundred and

---

22. Rev. 21:14

forty and four cubits, according to the measure of a man,
that is, of the angel.[23]

Why did the angel mention the gold and precious stones that were designed and built into the construction of this city?

It appears that the angel wanted John to know of the great wealth this city embodies, thus possibly signifying the great wealth each inhabitant of this city enjoys. In other words, the inhabitants of this city originally joined the Church of Jesus Christ, not for wealth, but to serve God and all mankind. But at the end, by being obedient to the commandments of Jesus Christ, they not only magnified their character attributes and developed lasting ties to family and friends, but were also rewarded with great wealth.

18 And the building of the wall of it was of jasper: and the city was pure gold, like unto clear glass.

19 And the foundations of the wall of the city were garnished with all manner of precious stones. The first foundation was jasper; the second, sapphire; the third, a chalcedony; the fourth, an emerald;

20 The fifth, sardonyx; the sixth, sardius; the seventh, chrysolite; the eighth, beryl; the ninth, a topaz; the tenth, a chrysoprasus; the eleventh, a jacinth; the twelfth, an amethyst.

21 And the twelve gates were twelve pearls; every several gate was of one pearl: and the street of the city was pure gold, as it were transparent glass.[24]

---

23. Rev. 21:15-17
24. Rev. 21:18-21

Why is there no temple in this city?

John did not see a temple because the temple was only a facility to help carry out God's work to bring to pass the eternal life of man. Since the individuals in this city have all achieved eternal life, there is no need for a temple.

> 22 And I saw no temple therein: for the Lord God Almighty and the Lamb are the temple of it.[25]

Who else will bring their glory into this city?

The tremendous brilliance of light that emanates from our Savior seems to be in direct proportion to His love, honor and wisdom. The light the Lord emanates is so bright that it lights up the whole city. John saw that the people who inhabit this city, from different nations, are fortunate to be able to benefit from the Lord's great qualities. John also saw that those righteous individuals who have been rewarded with their own kingships also bring their glory and honor into the city. Because of this light there is no darkness in this city and therefore, no need to shut the gates.

> 23 And the city had no need of the sun, neither of the moon, to shine in it: for the glory of God did lighten it, and the Lamb is the light thereof.
> 24 And the nations of them which are saved shall walk in the light of it: and the kings of the earth do bring their glory and honour into it.
> 25 And the gates of it shall not be shut at all by day: for

---

25. Rev. 21:22

there shall be no night there.
26 And they shall bring the glory and honour of the
nations into it.[26]

For those who live in this city what is the one thing they all have in common?

John was told that all must have had their names written in the book of life. And those that do not find their names in this book are they that defile or worketh any abominations such as, being profane, make corrupt, willing to blaspheme, hate mongering or maketh a lie.

27 And there shall in no wise enter into it any thing that
defileth, neither whatsoever worketh abomination, or
maketh a lie: but they which are written in the Lamb's
book of life.[27]

---

26. Rev. 21:23-26
27. Rev. 21:27

22

Blessings for the Righteous

Previously, an angel has been describing the construction and exquisite garnishments and decor of this great holy city. John was also shown how the righteous exist.

What are the waters of life and the trees of life?

John saw a pure river of water proceeding forth from the throne of God the Father and Jesus Christ. This water flows down the middle of a wide street. On either side of this river is a tree, called a tree of life. These two trees yield twelve crops of fruit, a different variety each month. The leaves of these trees are for the healing of the nations. It appears that the water, the twelve different types of fruit, and the leaves exist to provide needed sustenance for an immortal body to maintain its glorified nature. This is possible, because the water is called the water of life and the trees are called trees of life and the properties in the leaves provide rejuvenation. Like the walls, gates, and foundation, there is normally a secondary symbolic meaning attached to each item mentioned. The water could represent the Gospel which Jesus had compared to living waters. The fruit of the trees could be symbolic of the love of God, because if the Savior had not atoned for the sins of all mankind then none of the inhabitants of this city would even have the opportunity to partake of the water and different yields from trees of life.

> *1 And he shewed me a pure river of water of life, clear as crystal, proceeding out of the throne of God and of the Lamb.*
> *2 In the midst of the street of it, and on either side of the river, was there the tree of life, which bare twelve manner of fruits, and yielded her fruit every month: and the leaves of the tree were for the healing of the nations.* [1]

What is meant by the words, there shall be no curse?

In the garden of Eden, Adam and Eve were told by God that if they ate from the forbidden tree they would not only die, but the ground would be cursed so that in sorrow they would eat of it all the days of their lives. [2] Now that the saints have overcome, this curse is no longer in effect. All elements required

---

1. Rev. 22:1-2
2. Gen 2:17; 3:16; 17:19

for eternal life and happiness will be freely available. In addition, God the Father and Jesus Christ will have their thrones there, and in appreciation for being saved into the kingdom, the saints will want to serve the Father and the Lamb eternally.

> 3 And there shall be no more curse: but the throne of God and of the Lamb shall be in it; and his servants shall serve him:[3]

Whose face will they see?

John is told that the inhabitants of this city will see the face of Jesus Christ.[4] John also says that when we see the Savior, we shall be like him; for we shall see him as he is.[5]

> 4 And they shall see his face; and his name shall be in their foreheads.[6]

What is meant, "For the Lord God giveth them light"?

We already know that both God the Father and Jesus Christ emit a glorious light from their immortal bodies, but this seems to be saying that God will give those who reign with him light. In other words, their immortal bodies will also emit a similar form of light that will help light this holy city forever.

> 5 And there shall be no night there; and they need no candle, neither light of the sun; for the Lord God giveth them light: and they shall reign for ever and ever.[7]

---

3. Rev. 22:3   6. Rev. 22:4
4. Matt. 18:10   7. Rev. 22:5
5. 1 John 3:2

How does the angel conclude this vision to John?

He signifies the truthfulness of this vision. By bearing a final testimony that God did send him to show John those things which will come to pass.

> *6 And he said unto me, These sayings are faithful and true: and the Lord God of the holy prophets sent his angel to shew unto his servants the things which must shortly be done.[8]*

What warning is John told to pass on?

John is told to tell the world that the Savior will come suddenly and blessed is he that will respond to the warnings and the promises of this book.

> *7 Behold, I come quickly: blessed is he that keepeth the sayings of the prophecy of this book.[9]*

How did John surprise the angel?

As John began to hear these things he apparently mistook the angel for Jesus Christ and fell on his knees to worship him. The angel gently chides John for doing this by explaining that it is not appropriate, because he is only a fellow prophet who follows the teachings of Christ. In other words, John is told we don't worship angels, we only worship God.

> *8 And I John saw these things, and heard them. And when*

---

8. Rev. 22:6
9. Rev. 22:7

I had heard and seen, I fell down to worship before the feet of the angel which shewed me these things.
9 Then saith he unto me, See thou do it not: for I am thy fellowservant, and of thy brethren the prophets, and of them which keep the sayings of this book: worship God,[10]

Was John told to keep these prophecies secret?

On the contrary, John was told not to keep this information secret. That the time is at hand to give it to the world.

10 And he saith unto me, Seal not the sayings of the prophecy of this book: for the time is at hand.[11]

What will happen to the wicked who will never take the opportunity to repent?

John was told that at the final judgment those who are unjust will still be unjust, those who are filthy will still be filthy, those who are righteous will still be righteous and those who are holy will still be holy. In other words, the angel seems to be saying, who do you want your neighbors to be for the rest of eternity, the wicked or the just?

11 He that is unjust, let him be unjust still: and he which is filthy, let him be filthy still: and he that is righteous, let him be righteous still: and he that is holy, let him be holy still.[12]

What role does "works" play in the reward process?

---

10. Rev. 22:8-9
11. Rev. 22:10
12. Rev. 22:11

John was informed that the Savior will come suddenly, and when he comes each man would be judged according to his works whether they be good or bad.

> *12 And, behold, I come quickly; and my reward is with me, to give every man according as his work shall be.*[13]

What does the angel want everyone to know?

He wants all to know that Jesus Christ will personally testify that those who follow His commandments will have access to the holy city and the tree of life; but those who will not obey His teachings will be barred from entry into this city.

> *13 I am Alpha and Omega, the beginning and the end, the first and the last.*
> *14 Blessed are they that do his commandments, that they may have right to the tree of life, and may enter in through the gates into the city.*
> *15 For without are dogs, and sorcerers, and whoremongers, and murderers, and idolaters, and whosoever loveth and maketh a lie.*[14]

What does Jesus Christ want everyone to know?

He wants all to know that He has sent His angel to testify that these things are true.

> *16 I Jesus have sent mine angel to testify unto you these things in the churches. I am the root and the offspring of David, and the bright and morning star.*[15]

---

13. Rev. 22:12
14. Rev. 22:13-15
15. Rev. 22:16

What else does Jesus Christ want everyone to know?

He wants each of us to know that His gospel is available for anyone who wants to drink of the waters of eternal life.

> *17 And the Spirit and the bride say, Come. And let him that heareth say, Come. And let him that is athirst come. And whosoever will, let him take the water of life freely.*[16]

What will happen to someone who alters or changes the words in the Book of Revelation?

To anyone who changes the words of this book, the angel warns that God will give him the plagues of this book, then delete his name from the book of life and deny him access to the holy city.

> *18 For I testify unto every man that heareth the words of the prophecy of this book, If any man shall add unto these things, God shall add unto him the plagues that are written in this book:*
> *19 And if any man shall take away from the words of the book of this prophecy, God shall take away his part out of the book of life, and out of the holy city, and from the things which are written in this book.*[17]

What are the final words of the book?

The angel quotes the Savior's testimony that these words are true and again warns that He will come suddenly and then pronounces a final blessing upon all who read this book.

16. Rev. 22:17
17. Rev. 22:18-19

*20 He which testifieth these things saith, Surely I come
quickly. Amen. Even so, come, Lord Jesus.
21 The grace of our Lord Jesus Christ be with you all.
Amen.*[18]

What are the blessings promised to the seven churches?

When the Lord told John to write to the seven churches He
mentioned many blessings the saints would receive if they remained faithful to the end. Now that the angel has explained to
John what the righteous can expect to inherit the information
at the beginning of the Book of Revelation takes on more meaning. Listed below is a summary of the blessings that were promised to those individuals who, at the final judgement hear the
words, "Come, ye blessed of my Father, inherit the kingdom
prepared for you from the foundation of the world."[19]

- eat of the tree of life[20]
- receive a crown of life[21]
- shall not be hurt of the second death[22]
- eat of the hidden manna[23]
- be given a white stone[24]
- receive power over nations[25]
- receive the morning star[26]
- shall be clothed in white raiment[27]
- will have name in book of life[28]
- will hear Jesus Christ confess their name before God
  the Father [29]

18. Rev. 22:20-21   22. Rev. 2:11   26. Rev. 2:28
19. Matt. 25:34   23. Rev. 2:17   27. Rev. 3:5
20. Rev. 2:7   24. Rev. 2:17   28. Rev. 3:5
21. Rev. 2:10   25. Rev. 2:26   29. Rev. 3:5

- become a pillar in the temple of God[30]
- will carry the name of God[31]
- will inhabit the new Jerusalem[32]
- will sit with Jesus on His throne[33]

---

30. Rev. 3:12
31. Rev. 2:12

32. Rev. 3:12
33. Rev. 3:21